ALL YOU NEED
TO KNOW ABOUT
FENG SHUI

D1396657

ALL YOU NEED TO KNOW ABOUT
FENG SHUI

DR EVELYN LIP

Marshall Cavendish
Editions

Illustrations and text © Evelyn Lip
Photographs courtesy of Kenny Lip Yau Sueng

Editor: Lee Mei Lin / Designers: Bernard Go Kwang Meng and Benson Tan

Published by Marshall Cavendish Editions
An imprint of Marshall Cavendish International
1 New Industrial Road, Singapore 536196

Other Marshall Cavendish Offices:
Marshall Cavendish Ltd. 5th Foor, 32–38 Saffron Hill, London ECIN 8FH, UK • Marshall Cavendish Corporation. 99 White Plains Road, Tarrytown NY 10591-9001, USA • Marshall Cavendish International (Thailand) Co Ltd. 253 Asoke, 12th Flr, Sukhumvit 21 Road, Klongtoey Nua, Wattana, Bangkok 10110, Thailand • Marshall Cavendish (Malaysia) Sdn Bhd, Times Subang, Lot 46, Subang Hi-Tech Industrial Park, Batu Tiga, 40000 Shah Alam, Selangor Darul Ehsan, Malaysia

Marshall Cavendish is a trademark of Times Publishing Limited

National Library Board Singapore Cataloguing in Publication Data
Lip, Evelyn.
All you need to know about feng shui / Evelyn Lip. – Singapore : Marshall Cavendish Editions, c2008.
p. cm.
ISBN-13 : 978-981-261-593-0
1. Feng shui. I. Title.
BF1779.F4
133.3337 – dc22   OCN235706184

Printed in Singapore by Times Graphics Pte Ltd

To my son and daughter,
Kenny Lip Yau Sueng and Jacqueline Lip Tzun Cheang,
for their love and support

Contents

Foreword

There are many approaches to architecture from the functional to the intangible. Architects differ in their approaches and if architecture is the art of creating the living environment, then the approaches are limitless.

As one who has practised architecture for many years, I have frequently experienced feng shui through the agency of benign and knowledgeable clients who have successfully and constantly followed its precepts. In the world of Chinese Design Methods, whether building at a T-junction, at the foot of a hill or on a triangular site, a set of rules, as stringent as normal municipal building bylaws, have to be conformed with.

From feng (wind) to shui (water), one discerns the gaseous elements of the environment (air, wind, ventilation, air-conditioning) or its liquid aspects (rain, drainage, sanitation, dampness, waterproofing, rain-protection)—all within the ambit of normal solid architectural practice. Lao Tze the philosopher had suggested that the reality of a building does not consist in four walls and a roof but in the space enclosed.

I suggested to Evelyn Lip that she might look into the mass of information on the topic and perhaps suggest a guide for tyro architects and others on these intangible things which form a ponderable part of solid state architecture with or without architects. I wish her success in her search for meanings, and I am sure—like

The Bank of China stands out amidst many high-rises in the heart of Hong Kong. It was initially criticised for its sharp corners and cross bracings which are said to emit shaqi (overly excessive energy). On closer examination, it has good feng shui features, such as the ability to withstand hurricanes, and there is harmony in its Element of form.

acupuncture, bird's nest and shark's fin—it will create interest and provide food for thought in these seemingly imponderable things.

Professor E. J. Seow
(former Head, School of Architecture, University of Singapore,
in his Foreword to Chinese Geomancy, 29 March 1979)

Preface

From Professor Seow's Foreword to my first book *Chinese Geomancy – A Layman's Guide To Feng Shui*, it is clear that I was asked to research and write on the fascinating subject of feng shui in the late 70s.

At that time, books written in English on the methodology were not available. However, there were many written in classical Chinese and these were in the libraries. I was fortunate to be able to read the traditional text, and so I embarked on a personal journey of reading as many books as I could for a clear understanding of this ancient Chinese art that has survived thousands of years. This volume, *All You Need To Know About Feng Shui*, once again introduces the subject of feng shui but is presented with deeper insight and experience gained over the last two decades. It also updates the information presented in *Chinese Geomancy*.

Chinese Geomancy, published in 1979 by Times Books International, became a best-seller as soon as it was launched in the same year. I was constantly invited to speak to large audiences in Malaysia and Singapore, as well as overseas. In 1990, I presented a two-hour long lecture on feng shui and buildings at an international conference in Basel, Switzerland. I was one of the key speakers and the only Asian specialist on the subject of feng shui and the environment. As I addressed a crowd of over 4000 Westerners from various occupations, translators were present to render my speech into German, Swiss and French. One outcome of the conference was a book published in German, *Orte der Kraft-Krafte des Lebens*, in which I was featured. In the late 80s, the BBC interviewed me twice in Singapore, and in 1990 I was a guest on radio and television shows in nine cities in the United States. By the time my seventh book *Feng Shui For The Home* was published in 1985, other writers had already begun to publish on the subject of feng shui.

A good scholar of feng shui reads widely and comprehends how nature works, and thinks of ways to integrate feng shui with the physical and architectural environment. I hold a PhD and a Masters in Architecture, and have been applying the principles of feng shui in the course of my work as a full time lecturer in Architecture at the National University of Singapore until I retired in 1998. During that time, I was often engaged as a specialist consultant on feng shui and architecture for several mega projects.

I look at feng shui from many angles and apply not just the ancient theories and superstitious practices. In this technological age, it is of utmost importance to incorporate feng shui with architecture, environmental science, conceptual design, cultural heritage and interior decoration. For example, poor architectural design creates bad feng shui because tortuous circulation causes stress. Poor lighting and ventilation affect health. Such defects cannot be simply eliminated by placing a crystal in a corner of the building nor can they be corrected by hanging a mirror on a wall. Certainly, the feng shui of a building can be most effectively improved by proper orientation and siting in places that are favourable and have good qi (energy).

This book is written for men and women from all walks of life and professions, for designers and technocrats, architects and engineers, in fact anyone interested in understanding feng shui. The objectives can be summarised as follows: to explain feng shui; to reveal the principles of feng shui; to present some general rules governing the application of feng shui and the ideal feng shui model in landscaping, interior design, public and residential buildings; and finally to introduce the methodologies and ways of assessing feng shui.

The book is broadly divided into four parts and is illustrated with many of my own sketches, paintings and photographs, which help to integrate the tangible and intangible aspects of architecture. Part One presents an introduction to the subject of feng shui, an overview of available source materials and literature, and an explanation of the main feng shui principles.

The landscape around buildings, the shape and plan of the constructions and the colour schemes used in interior design are briefly introduced in Part Two of the book on Feng Shui Forms and Planning. With examples of residential, commercial and public buildings that illustrate how architecture and feng shui can work together, this section also describes some of the mythical origins behind some feng shui precepts.

Most interestingly, perhaps, is how the feng shui of a building can be assessed. Part Three of this book focuses on one methodology of feng shui practice, the Method School, and three approaches within it. Admittedly, the practice of feng shui is like the practice of all other forms of art and architecture, and maturity, exposure and experience in the art are prerequisites to successful practice and implementation.

Part Four presents the feng shui analysis of some interesting classical buildings from the East and West. The feng shui of the burial ground for imperial Ming and Qing rulers is also described to highlight the rule of thumb for auspicious burial sites.

Evelyn Lip
August 2008

Acknowledgements

Despite the intervening years since the publication of my first book on Chinese geomancy, I am still very much indebted to Professor E. J. Seow for his kind suggestion to carry out research on this very interesting topic.

The National Libraries in Singapore hold 66 of my books and papers on feng shui and architecture, most of them in the reference sections. I would like to thank the librarians and all readers who have given me recognition, encouragement, inspiration and moral support throughout the years. Special thanks go to Lily, Kon Sang, Margaret, Kee Wee, Swee Hoon, Agnas, Catherine, Lai Yoong and Cynthia.

I am, indeed, grateful to Chris Newson for his interest in republishing my books on feng shui. He is a man with vision and foresight. I am indebted to my editor Lee Mei Lin for her patient guidance, for being my mentor and editor, and for giving me valuable advice. I am also indebted to the many organisations and their representatives for allowing me to take photographs and describe their buildings in relation to feng shui practices.

Finally, I wish to thank my family members for their encouragement, support and constructive advice. In particular, I would like to acknowledge my cousin and his wife, Michael and Swee Mei, and my son and daughter, Kenny and Jacqueline.

Introduction

What is feng shui? What is its relevance to buildings? How does one practise feng shui? What is the architecture of feng shui buildings? This book aims to answer these and many other questions on feng shui. By adopting a practical and tangible approach, the mystery of an ancient art-form—one that has been safeguarded by the Chinese for centuries—will be unraveled; understanding of feng shui theory and practice will be heightened; and the reader will be left with a clear view of the discipline from an architectural perspective.

Feng shui, or Chinese geomancy, is the art of placement. It is a skill used to address the built and natural environments, and a knowledge that contributes greatly when dealing with the natural forces on earth. It is a complex subject involving many disciplines, ranging from site planning to psychology. A perfect feng shui model is said to be graced with *tianning, dili renhe* (heaven's blessings, which bring harmony and prosperity). Every individual, work place and nation needs to have auspicious feng shui for peace of mind, success and good fortune.

Zhong Hedian, the middle palace of the Forbidden City. Built in AD 1420, it faces south with its back against a man-made hill of coal, specially created to reduce negative energy.

The Chinese have always believed that one's success is determined by five factors, namely:

- *yiming* (destiny);
- *eryun* (the lucky and unlucky eras);
- *san feng shui* (the art of placement or feng shui);
- *shi daode* (virtue); and
- *wu dushu* (everything that concerns oneself, such as inheritance and family background, as well as everything one undertakes, such as education, experience and exposure).

The first two factors—*yiming* and *eryun*—are not within human control. It is therefore important to ensure that the third, fourth and fifth areas are not overlooked but rather developed to their maximum potential. With today's stressful working environment and highly competitive society, every ambitious person requires good feng shui for his living and work place. In the increasingly complex and competitive arena of international and local business, auspicious feng shui in the marketplace is needed more than ever before.

Everyone and every business establishment is housed in a building whose form and space, structure and finish, orientation and siting react with the forces of nature and are influenced by its environment. Educated clients of architects and builders have their own value system and ways of evaluating form, space and structure. However, in spite of technological advances, many people still regard feng shui as one of the most important aspects of design and planning. Thus, the architecture of a building must have close links with the positive workings of feng shui. The tangible aspects—such as space and form, lighting and ventilation, planning and circulation—must be complemented by the intangible aspects (feng shui) of architecture. The qi (energy) and magnetism of the earth, the symbolism of shapes with reference to the Five Elements, and the nature of the site must be in harmony with nature for the users to reap the benefits of auspicious feng shui.

With the greenhouse effect, deforestation and increasing global pollution, mankind must strive to adopt a more proactive attitude towards the preservation of the natural as well as the built environment. Feng shui, when practised in the correct manner, certainly helps man to respect site constraints, thereby achieving harmony and balance with nature. No wonder feng shui has evolved from a mere Oriental art of siting into an international medium and environmental tool for design on micro and macro scales. Renowned schools of architecture in major universities, such as Harvard, have produced PhD or Masters graduates who have carried out in-depth studies of feng shui. Learned scholars such as Joseph Needham and W. T. De Bary have written about this aspect of Chinese culture. Even the highly respected architect, Sir Norman Foster, designs with reference to feng shui precepts; for example, he moved two escalators of the Hong Kong and Shanghai Bank so that they did not confront the main door.

Part One

What is
Feng Shui?

Feng shui, or Chinese geomancy, is the art of placing a building on a site so that it is in harmony with other man-made structures and in balance with nature.

Feng shui originated in China a few thousand years ago where it was used for the orientation of homes and palaces as well as burial sites. Actually, feng shui is related to all the geographical features of the area in which a tomb is situated, and in many aspects is connected with building and architectural features. Feng shui stands for the power of the natural environment—the wind and the air of the mountains and hills, the streams and the rain, and the composite influences of the natural processes.

In traditional China, the concept of the location of buildings and dwellings held great importance, and even the construction of towns followed a prescribed siting, dimensioning and orientation. The principles were as follows: The front of the site should preferably face the south and should always have an unhindered view, which would include a stream or the sea. The back of the site should always face the north, and should be hilly or have a mountainous shield to ward off evil influences. The dead should be buried on a south-facing slope. Left then should be the east, and right, the west. In Beijing, where cold, dusty winds blow unrelentingly from the north, it is advantageous for buildings to have solid north-facing walls and to have the windows and doors facing south. A building would be equally protected from the cold wind if sheltered behind by a hill. Clearly, man's living environment is of great importance to his happiness and wellbeing.

The system of feng shui is made up of the breaths of nature as well as the mathematical forms of nature.

In feng shui, five factors govern the choice of where a burial place or building may be sited. These factors have to be seriously considered because they are believed to influence the future or fate of the people involved. The factors are:

- *long* (dragon), representing the location of the burial ground;
- *xue* (hole), but in geomancy it indicates the foundation of the tomb or building site;
- *sha* (sand); symbolising the surroundings or neighbouring environment of the site;
- *shui* (water); depicting the streams flowing through or bypassing the site; and
- *xiang* (representing the orientation or the direction of the site).

The words feng shui in Chinese mean 'the wind and the water'. The classical name for feng shui was *kanyu*, which means 'incorporating *tiandao* (the ways of the heavens) and *didao* (the ways of the earth)'. In ancient times, feng shui was regarded as a form of biogeography, and during the Qing dynasty (AD 1616–1911) feng shui practitioners were called *dili jia*, or geographers (*dili* means 'geography'). The art of feng shui became a professional skill during the Han dynasty (206 BC – AD 220) and feng shui specialists of the time were called *kanyu jia*. Sometimes, the *kanyu jia* are referred to as *dili jia*.

The feng shui of a site was always assessed with reference to cosmological, environmental and earthly happenings. Feng shui is thus a discipline deeply rooted in Chinese cosmology and embedded in Oriental culture. The ancient Chinese believed that the universe was made from the union of yin and yang elements and, indeed, that everything under the sky could be classified under these two elements. The earth, the moon, darkness, night, the female and the valley are yin. The heavens, the sun, light, day, the male and the hill are yang. *Wanwu* (everything under the sky) is symbolised by the signs of the *Tai Ji* (Extremity and Infinity), which is the symbol of perfect balance and harmony, and the Eight Trigrams.

Undoubtedly, the art of feng shui includes understanding the many facets of Chinese beliefs and culture, such as the application of the theory of yin and yang, Chinese philosophy, Chinese symbolism and the theory of magnetism.

However, although feng shui has stood the test of time and has been practised by the forefathers of the Chinese for almost 3000 years as an ancient art, its theory and practice are not as well documented as other forms of art. The rudiments of feng shui and the methodology of practice are closely guarded by those who are truly knowledgeable and misunderstood by those who have only a superficial understanding.

Figure 1 – The Tai Ji, the symbol of perfect balance and harmony

Figure 2 – A simple rendition of the Eight Trigrams

LITERATURE ON FENG SHUI

For centuries, Chinese scholars have investigated and written about the theory of feng shui. Literature dating back to the 5th century BC have been found; these record the choice of sites for new cities and include the *Shujing* (the Book of Documents) and the *Shijing* (the Book of Songs). And in the 3rd century BC, there existed a Chinese dictionary containing records of choosing sites for building purposes.

One of the earliest works that described the feng shui of burial places is the *Zhuanjing* (the Book of Burial), written by an East Jin scholar by the name of Guopu (AD 317–420). Emperors from the Five Dynasties (AD 907–960) to the Qing dynasty were buried in tombs on hilly sites facing the south. Dayu, the emperor of the Xia dynasty (2140 – 1711 BC), chose to be buried in Huiji, an auspicious site. Emperor Qin Shi Huang, who began preparations for his mausoleum soon after ascending the throne, chose the hilly northern part of Lishan as his final resting place. Auspiciously placed tombs from the Ming (AD 1368–1644) and Qing dynasties can still be visited today.

During the period of the Han dynasty, Bangui, author of *Hanshu* (records of the Han dynasty) and *Yiwen Zhi* (essays on art and literature) wrote and discussed the workings of the Five Elements and the harmony of yin and yang, while the scholars Dongzhong Shu, Liuxiang and Weinan Zi wrote about the productivity and the destructibility of the Five Elements.

Several books, such as *Songhai Yiwen Zhi* (records of literature of song) and *Xiangzhai Jing* (a feng shui classic), published during the Song dynasty (AD 960–1279), elaborated on the workings of the Five Elements and the theory of yin and yang. Other well known ancient literature includes *Huangdi Erzhai Jing* (on imperial residences), *Didian Zhaijing* (on the siting of buildings), *Kongzi Zhaijing* (a Confucian classic on house design), *Zhaijing* (on house design), *Weinan Zizhai Jing* (a classic on house design by Wei), *Bagua Zhaijing* (on the house and Trigrams), *Liushi Sigua Zhaijing* (on the house and Hexagrams) and *Wuxiao Zhaijing* (on the five rules of house design). *Zhaijing* illustrated the meaning of the 24 orientations in feng shui divinations. During the South Song era, the philosopher Zhu Xi (AD 1130–1200), spoke of feng shui as the art of landscaping. The 675th volume of *Gujin Tushu Jicheng* (records from ancient to present times), compiled during the Qing dynasty, also contained substantial information on feng shui theory.

A popular book, *Bazhai Mingjing* (the enlightening mirror of the eight houses), presents a system of feng shui based on the assessment of the birth date of the owner of the building. From this, the owner's *minggua* (horoscope) can be obtained, upon which the orientation of the building is determined.

Literature in English on feng shui, however, does not date back to ancient times. It was only in the last quarter of the 20th century that Western scholars and other people became aware of this Oriental practice, and were immensely interested in its theory and application. Joseph Needham specifically mentioned the art of feng shui in his 1954 publication, *Science and Civilization in China*. He recognised the fact that feng shui concerned the intangible aspects of Chinese architecture and was the result of the moulding influences of wind and water. My book *Chinese Geomancy* was the earliest written in English on the practice of feng shui and the design and orientation of buildings. Following this, several books were published on the feng shui of homes and other buildings.

THE FIVE ELEMENTS

The Five Elements is an important concept in feng shui. Comprising Wood, Fire, Earth, Gold and Water, it was introduced by the Chinese as early as the 4th century BC.

The sequence of these Elements was designed such that wood gives rise to fire, fire produces earth, earth gives birth to gold, gold creates water, and water makes wood. In other words, wood makes the fire, which burns it to ashes in the form of earth, which in turn contains gold in the form of ores. Gold produces water when condensation occurs, and gold can also be melted into a liquid state when heated. Water nourishes plants and trees, thus producing wood.

The ancient Chinese also believed in the power of counteraction between the Five Elements and that it was in accordance with the laws of nature and heaven. Thus water puts out fire, fire melts gold, gold breaks wood, wood cuts into the earth, and earth absorbs water. All calamities were said to arise from disturbances of the Five Elements, and the ancient Chinese were cautious not to interfere with the order of nature or cause disruptive disturbances to the natural conditions designed by heaven. The services of a geomancer were thus considered essential to determine the prevalence of the elements and forces.

Figure 3 – The diagrams show the productive (top) and destructive (bottom) relationship of the Five Elements.

The Five Elements are closely associated with matter and forces in nature:
* Wood is represented by the east, spring and the colour green;
* Fire by the south, summer and the colour red;
* Earth by the central position and the colour yellow;
* Gold by the west, autumn and the colour white; and
* Water by the north, winter and the colour black.

Just like the seasonal changes, the Five Elements work in cyclical motions and succeed one another in a cycle of either compatible or incompatible interaction. Compatible elements are: Wood with Fire, Fire with Earth, Earth with Gold, Gold with Water, and Water with Wood. Incompatible Elements are Earth with Water, Water with Fire, Fire with Gold, Gold with Wood, and Wood with Earth.

Table 1 The Five Elements and their characteristics

Element	Direction	Season	Colour	Compatible with
Wood	east	spring	green	Fire
Fire	south	summer	red	Earth
Earth	central	—	yellow	Gold
Gold	west	autumn	white	Water
Water	north	winter	black	Wood

THE EIGHT TRIGRAMS

The numerals of the Eight Trigrams are attributed to China's first legendary emperor, Fuxi (2852 BC). The ancient numerical symbols, which he discovered on the back of a mythical animal that came out of the Huang He (Yellow River), consisted of 55 black and white dots which were later used to form the Eight Trigrams. The numerals are made up of yin, a broken sign (- -), and yang, a continuous sign (—). Each solid line symbolises the dragon, which has always been recognised by the Chinese as a symbol of vigilance, strength and the virtues of Heaven. The number with one white dot was considered an odd and yang number, while the number with two black dots an even and yin number. Thus, 1, 3, 5, 7 and 9 are yang numbers (*tiandao*, associated with the heavens), and 2, 4, 6 and 8 are yin numbers (*didao*, associated with the earth). The number 9 is the supreme yang, and so it is associated with the supreme ruler, the emperor.

Each *gua* (Trigram) is made up of three numerals of either yin or yang, or a mixture of yin and yang. The Eight Trigrams are *qian, kun, zhen, kan, gen, xun, li* and *dui*, and they indicate the eight points of the *luopan*, the compass that geomancers use to determine orientation.

The relationship between the Eight Trigrams and feng shui can be summed up thus: When the Great Extreme or *Tai Ji* was formed, it produced the two

Figure 4 – The Eight Trigrams

complementary powers of yin and yang which gave birth to the four primary symbols that represent four of the Elements, namely Fire, Water, Wood and Gold. The Eight Trigrams which originated from these symbols determine the divination of fortune.

The geomancer determines the orientation of buildings or tombstones as he reads from the compass. The direction or orientation represented by the Eight Trigrams is as follows:

☰	qian	northwest; signifies the heavens and masculinity
☷	kun	southwest; represents the earth and femininity
☳	zhen	east; indicates change
☵	kan	north; indicates danger
☶	gen	northeast; refers to the mountains
☴	xun	southeast; refers to the wind
☲	li	south; associated with the sun, lightning and fire
☱	dui	west; signifies the clouds and moisture

By combining two signs or two Trigrams, a Hexagram is produced. And from the respective interactions of the eight signs of the Eight Trigrams (by multiplying the number 8 eight times), the 64 signs of the Hexagrams are formed (see Figure 5 on page 29).

Traditionally, the Eight Trigrams are Chinese systems of arrangements, and were given the names of Former Heaven Arrangement and Later Heaven Arrangement. Table 2 overleaf shows how the Eight Trigrams is related to the Five Elements, and how they are both associated with the animals and seasons.

Table 2 The Trigrams and their relation to the Elements, the animals and the seasons

Trigram	Direction	Element	Emblem	Associated animal	Associated season	Interpretation
qian	northwest	Gold	heaven	dragon, horse	late autumn	strength, roundness and vitality
kun	southwest	Earth	earth	mare, ox	late summer, early autumn	nourishment or squareness
zhen	east	Wood	thunder	galloping horse or flying dragon	spring	movement, roads or bamboo sprouts
kan	north	Water	moon and water	pig	mid-winter	curved things, wheels, mental abnormality, danger
gen	northeast	Earth	mountain	dog, rat, birds	early spring	gates, fruits, seeds
xun	southeast	Wood	wind	hen	late spring, early summer	growth, vegetative force
li	south	Fire	lightning	pheasant, toad, crab, snail, tortoise	summer	weapons, drought and brightness
dui	west	Water, Gold	sea-water	sheep	mid-autumn	reflections and mirror images

Confucius edited the *Yijing* (the Book of Changes), a work that spells out the hidden meaning of the ancient symbols of the Eight Trigrams and which fortune-tellers use for divining the future. Feng shui theory is indirectly related to the *Yijing* in the sense that the Eight Trigrams is used to denote the directions. The word *yi* represents the changing nature of all things and the interaction and relation of the yin and yang qualities of matter in nature. *Jing* means classic, thus the *Yijing* has been used as a classical reference for those seeking guidance and an improved quality of life in a technological world. In fact, the system used for modern computer programming is based upon the ancient numerals of yin and yang forming the 64 Hexagrams, which in turn form a binary coding.

Figure 5 – The 64 signs of the Hexagrams

Figure 6 – Trigrams from the Sui and Tang dynasties

THE TEN STEMS AND TWELVE BRANCHES

The Chinese calendar is based on the *Ganzhi* (Stems and Branches) system in which the *Tian Gan* (Ten Heavenly Stems) are combined with the *Di Zhi* (Twelve Earthly Branches) to form the cyclical 60 lunar recurrent years. The Ten Stems and the Twelve Branches were terms introduced by the Chinese before the Xia period (2140–1711 BC). Each Stem or Branch was related to the yin-yang principles. The *Ganzhi* system was devised so that each year is associated with an astrological animal symbol, namely Rat, Ox, Tiger, Rabbit, Dragon, Snake, Horse, Sheep, Monkey, Cock, Dog and Pig.

The Ten Stems are *jia, yi, bing, ding, wu, ji, geng, xin, ren* and *kui. Jia* means the sign of growth in spring and withering in winter. *Yi* indicates the triumph of life in spring or the spread of growth. *Bing* is the root of growth or blooming. *Ding* predicts the maturity of things that grow or the vegetation. *Wu* means that the growth has reached a stage of abundance and fullness. *Ji* is the order or hibernation of all things. *Geng* means the fullness leading to the need for change. *Xin* indicates freshness and restoration. *Ren*

Table 3 The Ten Stems and their significance

Stem	Significance	Example	Element
jia	sprouting	trees	Wood
yi	spread of growth	bamboo	
bing	blooming	flame	Fire
ding	maturity of things	light	
wu	abundance	mountains	Earth
ji	order of things	flat land	
geng	fullness	weapons	Gold
xin	restoration	utensils	
ren	height of function	bones	Water
kui	preparation for spring		

is the height of function and *kui* is the preparation for spring. In other words, the Ten Stems give the message of a chain reaction of nature where the growth begins in spring, reaches a stage of maturity, stops growing and renews itself. See Table 3.

The Chinese applied the names of the Twelve Branches for things related to the earth. The Branches are *zi, chou, yin, mao, chen, si, wu, wei, shen, you, shu* and *hai*. *Zi* indicates the bud or the young shoot of a plant; it also signifies the beginning of all things. *Chou* literally means tied, but actually it symbolises the growth of things. *Yin* literally means moved, but its significance is to lead the growing object and spread the growth. *Mao* is similar in meaning to the Stem, *wu*, as explained earlier. *Chen* symbolises progress and disregard for the old formation. *Si* means the renewed spirit. *Wu* is the stage of maturity, and *wei* signifies the smell of matured objects. *Shen* is the expanded form of maturity, while *you* means ripeness. *Shu* symbolises death and *hai* means nucleus. From this analysis, it is apparent that the Twelve Branches are fairly similar in meaning to the Ten Stems in that both express the chain reactions of nature.

Table 4 on page 32 shows the relationship between the Twelve Branches and the animal symbols. Table 5 on the same page shows the relationship between the Five Elements and the Ten Stems and Twelve Branches.

By combining the Branches and Stems, the sexagenary cycle was invented and applied to the Chinese calendar as early as the 3rd century BC by Emperor Qin Shih Huang's prime minister. The first year in each 60-year cycle consists of a Heavenly Stem and an Earthly Branch. For example, the year *Jiazi* is made up of *jia*, a unit of the Heavenly Stem, and *zi,* a unit of the Earthly Branch. The Stem *jia* is of Wood Element while the Branch *zi* is of Water Element.

Wang Anshi, a politician and philosopher of the North Song dynasty, presented a comprehensive picture of how various matter in nature and the affairs of man are associated with the Five Elements, and this is summarised in Table 6.

Table 4 *The relationship between the Twelve Branches and the animal symbols*

Branch	Animal symbol	Yin/Yang
zi	rat	yin
chou	ox	yin
yin	tiger	yang
mao	rabbit	yin
chen	dragon	yang
si	snake	yang
wu	horse	yang
wei	sheep	yang
shen	monkey	yin
you	cock	yang
shu	dog	yin
hai	pig	yin

Table 5 *The relationship between the Five Elements and the Ten Stems and Twelve Branches*

Element	Stem	Branch
Wood	jia, yi	yin, mao
Fire	bing, ding	si, wu
Earth	wu, ji	chou, chen, wei, shu
Gold	geng, xin	shen, you
Water	ren, kui	hai, zi

Table 6 *The Elements and their association with various matter in nature and the affairs of man*

Wood	Fire	Earth	Gold	Water
east	south	centre	west	north
spring, summer	late summer	autumn	winter	—
wind	heat	moisture	drought	cold
green	red	yellow	white	black
sour	bitter, sweet	bitter, sweet	salty	—
straight	sharp square	round	crooked	—
azure dragon	red bird	yellow dragon	white tiger	turtle
goat	rooster	ox	dog	pig
eye	tongue, mouth	nose	ear	—
anger	happiness	thinking	sadness	fear
muscle	pulse	flesh	skin, hair	bone

THE YIN AND YANG PRINCIPLES

The art of divination with regard to feng shui is closely related to the harmony of the cosmic breath—yin and yang. The *Encyclopedia Sinica* gives the following definition: "Yin and yang are the negative and positive principles of universal life." As early as the 6th century BC, the positive and negative qualities of the yin-yang principles were expressed on stone drums representing the dark and bright sides of a sunlit bank.

The theory of yin and yang is explained in the texts of *Daodi Jing* (classics of the Dao). Yin and yang elements are expressed as the dual components that make up the *Tai Ji*, the symbol of perfect balance and harmony. The *Tai Ji* duality refers to the yang sign of *tian* (the heavens) and the yin sign of *di* (the earth). From these, the Five Elements of Wood, Fire, Earth, Gold and Water are produced. Associated with the Elements are the Eight Trigrams as shown in the illustrations on page 34.

There is yin and yang in everything. When there is more yin than yang, it is classified as yin. When there is more yang than yin, it is considered yang. The precepts of yin and yang are contained in the *Zhuanjing* (the Book of Burial). This classic work states that the good energy of the earth is retained by water but dispersed by wild wind. However, when anything is too yin, it becomes yang and vice versa. For example, the day is hottest at noon and becomes less hot at 4:00 pm. By 8:00 pm it is cool. The day will be coolest at midnight only to gradually become warmer as the new day dawns. This is how yin-yang works. Similarly, the four seasons change from Spring (less yin) to Summer (yang) then to Autumn (less yang) and then to Winter (yin).

The yin-yang theory and the workings of the Five Elements are central to Chinese thinking. It is applied to all things Chinese, such as medical practices, food classification, martial arts and fine arts. Everything can be classified. Achieving a balance of yin, yang and the Five Elements in the built and natural environments is central to feng shui precepts. In the physical and the natural worlds, all things must be in balance and harmony to benefit man. Therefore, the positioning of buildings, the siting of trees and man-made elements, even the placement of doors and furniture, must be well thought out to channel good energy into the interior of the building. Yin and yang colours must also be used to bring about balance and contrast.

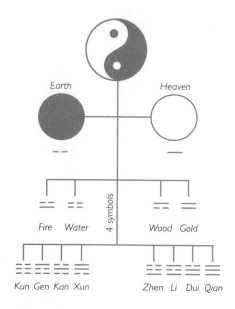

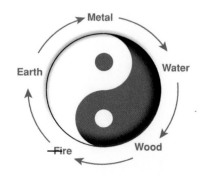

Figure 7 (left) – The Taiji duality refers to the yang sign of tian (the heavens) and the yin di (the earth). From these, the Five Elements are produced.

QI, HILLS AND WATER

Qi is the energy of the earth and comes in many forms. There is *shengqi* (vibrant energy; *sheng* means 'living' or 'alive'); *yangqi* (sun energy) and *yinqi* (moon energy); *tuqi* (energy from the ground) and *diqi* (earth energy); *chengqi* (moving energy) and *juqi* (conjoining energy). There is also *siqi* (stifling energy) and *shaqi* (overly or excessively vibrant energy).

Qi can also be classified as being heavenly, earthly and human. Heavenly qi is related to astronomy, cyclical timing, climatic and seasonal changes, as well as the natural forces such as wind and rain. Earthly qi is that related to the earth's topography and magnetic forces and earthly features such as the natural and built forms in the environment, space and structure, colours and lighting. Personal disposition, habit, nature and sensitivity of a person may be classified as humanly qi, which can be influenced by cultural and social factors.

Qi exists in the land and can be detected as undulating hills and landforms with high and low levels. It is closely linked with *li* (shape of land). The theory of *liqi* (the energy of the earth as expressed by the form) was discussed in Song dynasty writing by the philosopher Zhu Xi (AD 1130–1200). Classical works, such as the *Shanhai Guan* (the Pass of Shanhai) and the *Kaogongji* (the Records of the Arts), also state the feng shui situation of hilly sites. Hilly landforms spell the *longmo* (dragon vein) or the qi of the earth.

Mountain ranges of impressive height exert the yang energy, while low hilly sites express the yin force.

To the feng shui practitioner, the 'dragon' is the most significant factor as it either makes or destroys the fortune of man. It is the symbol of the beneficial forces of nature and the Superior Being. In feng shui, the 'twists and turns' or the 'ups and downs' of the body of the dragon represent the topography of the site. A 'false' dragon means that the land is flat, while a 'real' dragon is land that has a good undulating profile. A 'good' profile means that the site is of solid ground and favourable.

The Chinese recognise that the Kunlun Shan—consisting of five individual ranges, three of which are in China—is the most powerful range of mountains in China. These three notable 'dragons' spread from north to south. The north range backs onto the Huang He; the central range enhances the waters of Changjiang; the southern range spreads across the provinces of Yunnan, Guizhou, Guangxi, Guangzhou, Hunan, Fujian and Zhijiang. Other famous mountains in China noted for their excellent feng shui include the Hengshan, the Huashan, the Taishan and the Lushan, which is most imposing and noted for its breathtaking views and rejuvenating qi.

One example of a powerful man-made landscape is the Great Wall of China just outside Beijing at the Shanhai Guan in the province of Heibei. This imposing structure gives off good qi as it runs along undulating landforms with breathtaking views.

In feng shui terms, the most desirable situation is *fuyin baoyang, beishan mianshui* (there is yin and yang, hills in the rear and water in the front). It has been established that a good feng shui site must have the yin and the yang elements, the hill and the water, *diqi* (earth energy) and *shengqi* (vibrant energy). Most of the world's great cities are situated either on hilly sites with a mountain range as a backdrop, or are located by the sea or on the banks of beneficial rivers.

Water is a beneficial feature because it retains qi. However, this energy can be dispersed by very strong wind. Rivers must be long and winding, and the flow of water must pass by the front of the building. Although rivers are sources of qi, they can be destructive if they are too shallow or their flow too forceful. Rivers that tend to flood their banks should be moderated or controlled by engineering works. The Huang He, for example, was known in ancient times to cause floods; it was regarded as a poor feng shui element until its waters were channelled away to reduce excessive qi. Because rivers exert influence on buildings that are located on their banks, the relationship between the flow of the river and the siting of buildings may be favourable or unfavourable. Apart from rivers, lakes and ponds are also good sources of qi but the water must be calm and clear. Water is undesirable when it stagnates and emits a bad smell.

The Chinese saying *qi shi wan mu zhi yuan* (qi is the source of all things) echoes another saying *qi xing ce shui chu, shui zhi ceqi zhi,* which means 'when there is qi, water flows, but when water stops flowing, qi has been exhausted'. It is of vital importance that the main areas of living and working are located where qi is strong. This must have been why the ancients usually engaged a geomancer to determine the position of *shengqi* or vibrant energy before they began construction work on a building site.

FENG SHUI INSTRUMENTS

There are two schools of feng shui, each using its own methods. One, the Method School, makes use of the *luopan* (geomancer's compass) and methods of calculation. The Method School is also known as the Ancestral Hall or Direction Method. The other school is the Form School, also known as the Jiangxi Method. The Form

School relies largely on the assessment of landforms and acquired experience. The Method School is described in more detail in Part Three of this book.

The *luopan* (geomancer's compass)

In the Method School, the *luopan* is an important instrument for finding the direction and orientation of a building, the qi location and the relationship of the orientation with the stars. This method emphasises the relationship of the planets with the Eight Trigrams. There is a yin and yang for all things. If harmony of yin and yang elements is not achieved, they destroy each other. For example, if a thing or a part of nature is of yin, it must face the yin direction.

The Jiangxi Form Method is based on the understanding of the landscape, such as the profiles of the land (the advance or retreat of the 'dragon', i.e. the ups and downs of the profile of the land), the terrain (ground must be hard and solid and have a good profile like that of the real dragon) and water sources. In this method, the *luopan* is also employed to determine the orientation of a dwelling or to find a suitable burial site.

The first compass was invented during the Han dynasty (206 BC – AD 220). It was called *piao* (floating or rotating) because it consisted of a magnetic spoon which could freely rotate but always settled due north. Drawings found in Confucian classics show geomancers examining the ground conditions with instruments that resemble the modern-day geomancer's compass.

From this simple magnetic compass arose the *luopan,* which was devised to locate the qi of the earth. Early *luopans* were simple and contained 24 directions derived from the Ten Heavenly Stems and the Twelve Earthly Branches. More elaborate *luopans* were developed, comprising several concentric circles that contained the directions represented by the Eight Trigrams, the Five Elements, the Ten Heavenly Stems and the Twelve Earthly Branches. Over time, the *luopan* developed further into a complicated 36-tiered compass, which gave indications of space and time in geomantic assessments.

The modern-day *luopan* is made up of the *tianpan* (heaven's pool), the *dipan* (earth's pool) and the *renpan* (man's pool), and is mounted on a red board. Its central ring, the *tianpan,* contains a south-pointing magnetic needle used to detect locations with reference to watercourses; the *dipan* is used to locate the qi, commonly known

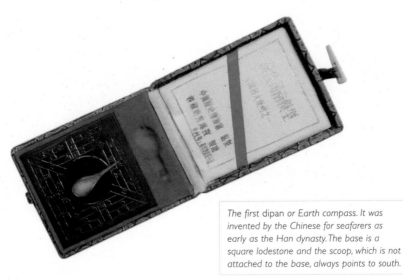

The first dipan or Earth compass. It was invented by the Chinese for seafarers as early as the Han dynasty. The base is a square lodestone and the scoop, which is not attached to the base, always points to south.

as the dragon, of the site; and the *renpan* is used to assess the topography of land. In all the three pools, 24 directions are marked using the names of the Heavenly Stems, the Earthly Branches and the Eight Trigrams.

Luopans differ in their design and detail, and it is beyond the scope of this book to discuss how they vary. Each type is to be read with particular reference to the maker's instruction manual. Most *luopans*, however, are discs of lacquered wood set into a square base. New models may come with a metal casing or finish, while cheaper ones are mounted on a plastic base. The discs are usually black overlaid with gold or red Chinese

(left) This luopan *is simple enough for the layman to use. Stand in the centre of a space and simply align the magnetic needle to north. Look at the readings: the red numbers are good but the black numbers are inauspicious. (right) Professional geomancers use more complicated* luopans *such as the one shown here.*

characters. Red strings or plastic threads divide the disc into four areas to show the four orientations of the object or building.

Geomancers take great care when using the *luopan*. So as not to get distorted readings, they do not place or read the instrument near magnetic objects and reinforced beams or columns. If necessary, they will crosscheck the reading with the reading of another compass.

The *lupan chi* (geomancer's ruler)

Apart from the orientation of a building and its doors, the size of the rooms and furniture within and the overall dimensions of a building are also carefully checked. For this, the *lupan chi* (the ruler of Lu Pan) is used. Believed to have been created by the well-known craftsman, Lu Pan, in the Lu State of the Chunqiu era (722 BC – AD 481), the geomancer's ruler is divided into eight parts, some of which are auspicious, others not. Some auspicious dimensions are as follows: doors should be 86 cm, 88 cm or 107 cm high or wide (main doors, 108 cm or 125 cm); corridors, 108 cm or 146 cm; ceilings, 300 cm or 320 cm; width of room, 300, 320, 368, 390, 408, 428, 448, 468 and 495 cm. The ruler should be used for measuring the main door and the more important furniture, such as the table that is to be used by the head of the company.

The drawing on page 42 shows the *lupan chi* specially made to measure (43 cm × 5 cm) and reduced to a scale of 1:4. It is divided into eight parts and each part is subdivided into four sections. The first part (reading from right to left) is *cai* (prosperity) while the last is *ben* (origin). Both are considered fortunate markings. The dimensions believed to bring fortune and wealth are multiples of 43 cm. The second part is *bing* (illness).

本	害	劫	官	義	離	病	財

Illustration of the geomancer's ruler

Any dimension that falls into this section spells a bad omen, such as losing a marriage partner, job or fortune. The third part is *li* (separation). Again this conveys the presage of bad luck and separation. The fourth is *ee* (righteousness) which predicts prosperity, posterity and security. The fifth, *guan* (official), is a sign of good fortune, eminence and promotion. The sixth, *jie* (robbed) denotes an extremely unfortunate prediction as it spells death, misfortune and separation. The seventh, *hai* (harm) foretells calamity, death, illness and quarrel.

CONCLUSION

In this technological age, how should man practise feng shui? Consultancy work requires the geomancer to apply his or her knowledge of science, architecture and the rudiments of feng shui to produce a harmonious union of the tangible and intangible aspects of architecture and feng shui. The discipline is so deeply rooted in Chinese architecture that its principles and rudiments were applied to imperial palaces and important buildings throughout the last few dynasties and kingdoms of China. For example, the imperial palaces in the Forbidden City of Beijing were built entirely based on the traditional concepts of feng shui. In my book *Feng Shui in Chinese Architecture*, the principles of Chinese architecture, complete with the assessment and analysis of the feng shui of the Forbidden City, are presented.

Form and colour depict nature or Element. The round form is of Gold Element, triangulated form is Fire Element and water is free form. In this painting, the starfruits are symbols of Fire (sharp edges) and Earth (yellow), and so form and colour are in harmony. As for the apples, green is Wood and red is Fire, and thus they are also in harmony. This is a picture that depicts harmony and can be hung in the south wall of the dining room.

Part Two

Feng Shui Forms and Planning

While it is important to capture the good qi of a site, whether for living or working purposes, it is also vital to mould the structure's *xue* (form) and space so that it is beneficial for man. In this respect, the site and its surrounding environment, and the interior spaces—down to the planning, design and finish—are equally important when evaluating the feng shui of a place. The importance of this is implied in section 670 of the Qing dynasty work, *Gujin Tushu Jicheng* (records from ancient to present times).

AN IDEAL FENG SHUI MODEL

The Chinese have long since established an ideal feng shui model. For example, in a location where the cold north wind blows, it is best to have a hill at the rear and north, and a lake in front. In addition, the ground on the left should be higher than the ground on the right. The left is regarded as the site of the Azure Dragon, one of the four symbols derived from the *Tai Ji* and which represents the physical features on the left side of a site, while the right is the site of the White Tiger. In Chinese mythology, the Azure Dragon and the White Tiger are protective symbols.

Qi is the empty and the void, and as it cannot be seen, the qi of a place is intuitive and intangible. On the other hand, the *xue*, being the foundation as well as the built-

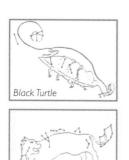

The celestial sphere is divided into four heavenly quadrants comprising the Black Turtle (north), the Azure Dragon (east), the White Tiger (west) and the Red Bird (south). The quadrant positions are analogous with the earthly feng shui models.

up areas, is physical and tangible. For example, in a traditional Chinese house where there is a central *mintang* (courtyard), qi is equated with the courtyard, while *xue* is the built-up or interior space of the house. The ideal house (and even the ideal burial site) is supposed to have both a courtyard, so that qi is not blocked, and a built-up *xue*. The relationship of this *xue* with the surrounding landscape and the Five Elements is of importance to the feng shui of the structure. Even the location of the main entrance to the *xue* is also important, as mentioned in the *Gujin Tushu Jicheng*.

The form and shape of a structure can be classified under the following five pairs of Elements:

- Water (intuitive or free form) with Wood (elongated or rectangular);
- Wood with Fire (triangular);
- Fire with Earth (square);
- Earth with Gold (round); and
- Gold with Water (free form).

The combination of various forms and shapes that a structure takes should be made with reference to the Element of the form or shape. Examples of auspicious and inauspicious combinations can be seen in Figures 8 to 11. Figures 12 to 16 are examples of some older architectural structures from Europe and a brief assessment of their Elements.

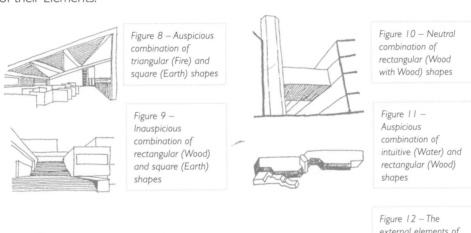

Figure 8 – Auspicious combination of triangular (Fire) and square (Earth) shapes

Figure 9 – Inauspicious combination of rectangular (Wood) and square (Earth) shapes

Figure 10 – Neutral combination of rectangular (Wood with Wood) shapes

Figure 11 – Auspicious combination of intuitive (Water) and rectangular (Wood) shapes

Figure 12 – The external elements of St Paul's Cathedral in London are made up of shapes of many Elements: Gold, Fire, Wood and Earth. On the other hand, the plan is made up of spatial forms of mainly Gold and Earth Elements.

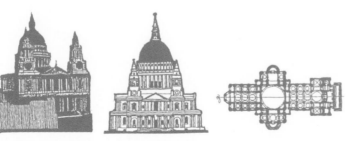

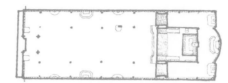

Figure 13 – Le Raincy
Notre Dame, Paris,
was also designed in
plan as Wood Element.
And in perspective,
its Wood Element is
complemented by the
Fire Element.

Figure 14 – The
compatible Elements of
shape, Wood and Fire,
are often used in bridge
designs. A good example
is the Salginatobel
Bridge in Switzerland,
designed by Robert
Maillart, as shown in the
drawing on the left.

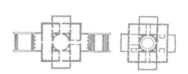

Figure 15 – Mereworth
in Kent, England, has a
central space of Gold
Element, and an outer
interior space of Earth
Element. Earth produces
Gold, and so the
Elements are in harmony.

Figure 16 – The elevational treatment
of Queen Square, Bath, designed
by John Wood the Elder, consists of
shapes of Fire and Wood Elements.

So far I have presented buildings that were built or renovated many years ago. What about the buildings of today? Has feng shui been applied to them, resulting in changes to their overall design and internal structure? Without a doubt, yes.

I have been engaged by building owners to advise on the feng shui of several projects. In a project I did in Singapore at the end of 1989, when the plans for a multi-storeyed business centre were presented at the initial stage, four huge columns could be seen on the front facade. I noticed that the span of the columns was tremendous, and that the supporting structural members, beams and columns were huge. Not only that, the mailroom was next to the main entrance. By the time that first meeting ended, the design was much improved. The facade was streamlined to have six elegant columns, which allowed for better circulation and use of spaces.

This leads me to bring up a very important point in the practice of feng shui. There is more to just knowing all the rules of thumb of feng shui and being able to use the *luopan*. Let me explain.

- Vital knowledge includes the ability to identify the user's Birth Element. As one's Birth Element is said to determine one's destiny, knowing the Birth Element means that the building and its spaces can be oriented to complement the user's character and nature. Information on Birth Element can be found in my companion book, *Personalise Your Feng Shui And Transform Your Life*.

- One should ideally have some knowledge, if not expert knowledge, of interior design, the aesthetics of design, and the architectural treatment of spaces and forms so as to be able to see the problems and suggest viable solutions.

- One must be conscious of the built environment and the surrounding landform.

As early as the 3rd century BC, the Chinese were already very sensitive to the forces and topographic features of nature, and would address them respectfully. For instance, they constructed the Great Wall along the undulating nature of the terrain, and in so doing the wall meandered according to the twists and turns of the land. Being sensitive to the terrain meant working in harmony with nature. If the terrain were not respected, disasters such as landslides and loss of human lives would occur. One can achieve good feng shui through good site and architectural planning and even harmonious interior design, in fact everything else that is related to comfort and harmony.

- Feng shui is a multi-faceted discipline. When a building is in harmony with nature and other structures in its vicinity, it is auspicious feng shui in terms of siting. When a building design is evolved organically and it fulfils practical needs and cultural aspirations, it scores an important mark in the assessment of feng shui. When an interior is created as a tactile harmonious living space, it is an environment with good feng shui.

To illustrate these points, I present brief studies of six modern iconic buildings. Some of these structures may not have been designed with input from feng shui experts. However, when architects regard the power of natural forces very seriously, they succeed in creating buildings that withstand the test of time and the ravages of nature. Some buildings are related to nature; the Sydney Opera House, for instance, resembles the petals of flowers unfolding to the sea, an image that depicts natural growth. Some say it looks like sea shells reaching out in two directions.

The curved, white sea shell-like roof structures of the
Sydney Opera House are Gold Element in essence
and are thus in harmony with the water.

Symbolism also plays a role in the design of feng shui buildings. Many world-
renowned mega buildings are 88 storeys high, simply because the Cantonese regard
8 as a lucky number and 88 implies even more fortune. One example is the Jin Mao
Tower in Pudong, Shanghai's new business centre. Designed to be a highly intelligent
building, its 88 storeys are equipped with the latest technology.

And of course, the location of buildings—where they are sited—is of vital
importance in garnering good feng shui. For example, it is not good practice to place
a building at a Y- or a T-junction. A structure like the Arc de Triomphe in Paris sits at
the centre of eight road junctions that radiate from it, and the energy of the site is
very vibrant. Buildings that take on a triangular shape (Fire Element) are also charged
with energy. A tall metal structure like the Eiffel Tower is charged with vibrant energy.
No wonder it has been regarded as a symbol of romance in Paris.

Transamerica Corporation Building, San Francisco

San Francisco's Transamerica Corporation Building, its triangular shape depicting the Fire Element, was built to withstand earthquakes. In the earthquake of 1989 with its magnitude of 7.1, the structure shook for a minute or so but was undamaged. All those precautions taken at the design stage has meant good feng shui for the building.

National Stadium and National Theatre, Beijing

The National Stadium in Beijing is an example of good feng shui siting. It is situated on a slope and on undulating ground with good qi. Constructed in 2008 for the Beijing Olympic Games, the design concept could have been inspired from bird's nests that are commonly seen in nature. Surrounding the stadium, to the east and north, are lakes. East, which is of Wood Element, and north, which is of Water Element, are intrinsically in

The structure of Beijing's National Stadium, being intuitive and spanning from many directions, is of Water Element and is harmonious with the overall plan, which is basically of Gold Element.

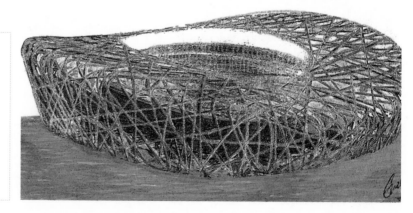

*The Transamerica
Corporation
Building, San
Francisco, USA*

The National Theatre, Beijing

harmony with the lakes, which are of Water Element. Other commendable feng shui features are its good acoustic design and the naturally ventilated interior.

About 500 metres from the famous Tiananmen Square lies the Zongguo Guojia Dajuchang, Beijing's new National Theatre. This unique structure, with a titanium shell opening that unfurls like a curtain, takes on the shape of an elliptical dome (Gold Element). The entrance to the theatre is through a tunnel under a man-made pool, which makes the theatre appear to float. It is in harmony with nature and the feng shui is good as the Gold Element in its shape is in harmony with the Water Element of the pool.

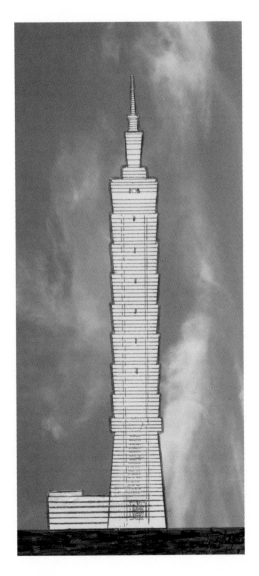

Taipei 101, Taiwan

The Taipei 101 (left) is another example of a building constructed to withstand natural disasters. Completed in 2004 and standing at an imposing 509.2 metres tall, it was the tallest structure in the world then. The building boasts several excellent feng shui features. For instance, the foundations as well as the superstructures were designed to withstand strong earthquakes and gale winds, which meant it has been able to resist devastating hurricanes.

The structure also wields auspicious symbolism. Each tier of the tower contains eight floors, which, in the Cantonese dialect sounds like *fa* (becoming rich). In addition, symbols of the *ruyi* (having your wishes come true) were applied on each tier on all sides of the facade. The emperors of the Ming and Qing dynasties often awarded *ruyi* to government officials in the form of jade in auspicious symbolic designs.

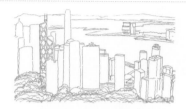

Figure 17 – Sketch plans of the Bank of China; (opposite) The Bank of China

GROUND FLOOR

SKETCH: 38TH FLOOR PLAN

70TH FLOOR PLAN

Bank of China, Hong Kong

When the Bank of China was completed in 1989 at the flourishing centre of Hong Kong, it was criticised for having many sharp corners confronting the other buildings that surround it. At 315 metres tall, it was once the tallest building in Hong Kong. Designed by world-renowned architect, I. M. Pei, this 70-storeyed asymmetrical expression of uniqueness and elegance is a good example of architectural masterpiece. Geometry plays an important part in the elevational as well as the structural expressions.

This strikingly modern building comprises a square plan (Earth Element), and its elevational geometry is mainly composed of triangles (Fire Element). Fire produces Earth, and so the Elements are in harmony. Inspired by the elegance of bamboo and its growth pattern, the architect let the building emerge from a cube with shafts rising from it to symbolise growth. This symbolism is good feng shui. A sketch of the floor plan shows the main structural columns at the four corners. Sketch plan of the 38th floor shows the 5th column which gives it additional strength and power. This fascinating building stands out amidst many high-rise buildings in the heart of Hong Kong.

Esplanade Theatres On The Bay, Singapore

Sited on the north bank of Marina Bay, Singapore's sophisticated performing arts venue is indeed unique as a piece of architecture. Soon after it was completed and opened to the public, I commented on its feng shui in a television interview.

The site is auspicious. The Esplanade is located in quite a central position with many important complexes nearby. On the left of the site, represented by the bay, is the Azure Dragon, a mythical protective guardian that always sits on the left of sites. There is good circulation in and around the building for pedestrians and concertgoers, and an efficient vehicular network system. Architecturally, the Esplanade Theatres On The Bay is a juxtaposition of transparent and opaque treaments. A sketch of the site plan is shown opposite.

The architects of the project used two cladding shells over the main theatres, each of which carry thousands of triangulated sun-shading hoods. These hoods are of the Fire Element. However, the colour of the material used for them is of Gold Element. As such, there is no real harmony here. On the other hand, the shape of the theatres, which is more related to the Gold Element, is in harmony with the bay (Water Element).

Most importantly, the performance spaces within are acoustically sound and this in itself is good feng shui. Good acoustics is good feng shui because a theatre or concert hall can only be effective with excellent acoustics. When performance halls are effective, patrons and crowds can be expected and business is good. This is not surprising as the builders engaged the services of the renowned acoustician Russell Johnson of American firm, Artec Consultants. The theatre for orchestral and opera performances is decorated in red and gold, which are of Fire and Earth Element respectively. This is good as the colours are in harmony.

The Esplanade Theatres On The Bay, with its distinctive sun-shading hoods.

Figure 18 – Sketch plan of the site

Swiss Re Headquarters, London

Some new buildings are aerodynamic and induce good natural ventilation through remarkable design and planning. These buildings have fulfilled a few areas with regards to feng shui requirements. One good example is the Swiss Re Headquarters (below). Built in 2004 in London's financial hub, it is an example of good planning with excellent building science features. It is circular in plan and depicts the Gold Element. A commendable feature that echoes good feng shui practice is that it is ecological and facilitates effective natural ventilation. Its pine cone-like shape is resistant to wind and noise, and this is a good feng shui feature.

FENG SHUI GARDENS AND LANDSCAPE

Chinese gardens and landscape design is unique and very different from Western styles in that the underlying concept is based on intuition and freedom. Unlike the formal and systematic approach adopted in the West, Chinese garden design is based on the feng shui precepts of harmony and the contrast of yin and yang.

Chinese landscape gardens are incomplete without spaces modelled on Confucian and Daoist ideas. Confucian precepts are based on balance and symmetry while Daoist ideas are free flowing and intuitive. A feng shui landscape garden is like a Chinese brush painting, and the gardens are created to express *chang* (hidden) and *lu* (exposed) areas, as well as *she* (void) and *shi* (solid) areas. The criteria include the creation, grouping or dispersal of elements of design; creating rhythm in the design of spaces; creating a sense of light and shade; creating differences in levels of pavements and floors of buildings; creating perspectives and borrowed vistas; and finally, creating a sense of balance and harmony.

There must be yang elements, such as rocks or hills, and yin elements, such as water or shaded areas. Unlike rockeries or hills, which are solid elements, streams, rivers and lakes are fluid and intuitive, giving qi and life to the garden landscape. There must also be large open spaces contrasting small semi-covered spaces; built-up areas and open courtyards; covered walkways and exposed paths; arched bridges and connecting zigzagged walkways; tall structures, such as pagodas, and low-rise or single-storey pavilions next to rockeries. A Chinese landscape garden must present not only interesting views but also a sense of anticipation, peace and tranquility.

To enhance the spatial concept of a garden, the landscape designer makes use of high and low land, inserts man-made water sources to enhance qi, and introduces rockeries and plants to create harmony and balance. The planting of trees and the siting of ponds, rocks and bridges are carried out with reference to the Element or the location of the site. For example, if the position of the site is south, which is related to the Fire Element, there should not be ponds or lakes. On the other hand, the north and northwest, being related to the Water Element, are good places to introduce pools, ponds or other water features.

Willow trees are best planted along the side of ponds because its leaves and even its branches are 'soft' like the Water Element, and so they are in harmony with the water in the ponds. Rockeries should provide a backdrop to the setting and contrast with the pond. Flowers, plants and trees are decorative and bring life and colour to the garden. Yin trees (trees that produce cool-coloured fruits or flowers) are best located in the north, while yang trees (trees that bear warm- or red-coloured fruits or flowers) should be in the south. Bridges should link sources of qi and should be curved, arched or zigzagged to reduce *shaqi* (overly vibrant energy).

Ponds, rockeries and pavilions are important components in Chinese gardens.

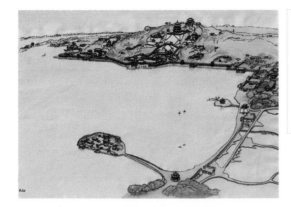

Sketch of Yi Heyuan (Summer Palace). In the foreground lies the South Lake Island, which sits on the Kun Minghu (Kunming Lake) and faces Wan Shoushan (Longevity Hill). Pavilions and other structures were built on the little island in the traditional style raised on solid rocks. This island was purposely created to complement the feng shui of the hill, which is the focal point of the Summer Palace.

The calm water of the Kun Minghu reflects the natural and architectural form of Longevity Hill. Originally called Golden Water Pond, the lake was enlarged in the 12th century. Sited on the hill is the striking 40-metre timber tower, the Fo Xiangge (Pavilion of the Buddha's Fragrance).

FENG SHUI COLOURS AND INTERIOR DESIGN

The Chinese believe colours have a certain meaning and symbolism. Red represents joy and good fortune; yellow, royalty and prominence; green, longevity and youthfulness; blue, spiritualism and heavenly blessings; black, sadness and sombreness; and white, mourning and purity. Traditionally, these colours have been applied on Chinese buildings to reflect the wishes of the people. For example, the Tiantan (Temple of Heaven) was covered by a three-tiered blue tiled roof because it was for the worship of the heavens, and the emperors of the Ming and Qing dynasties called upon the heavenly gods to give their blessings for a good harvest. See page 110 for more on the Tiantan.

Because the feng shui expert deals with space, form and structure, he should also be a sensitive interior designer. His sensitivity and awareness of the built interior helps him to improve a poor feng shui design. In planning an interior with good feng shui, the geomancer should be fully conscious of what he sees from all possible angles within the confines of the interior space. Where renovation work is required, he has to identify the defects of the interior in terms of feng shui and other design considerations that affect the wellbeing of the occupants. Here, he looks into the composition of form and space, the patterns and textures of furnishing materials, and also the colour scheme.

The colours used must enhance the interior and create a contrast with the exterior. The geomancer does not simply use colour to emphasise form and space, he uses it to create symbolism and a balanced interior. For good feng shui, the colour scheme should be harmonious—neither overpowering (too yang) nor too monochromatic (too yin). Furthermore, the colours should be compatible with the user's Birth Element (more information on the Elements of Birth is presented in *Personalise Your Feng Shui And Transform Your Life*). Once an analysis has been made and the appropriate hue decided, two tints of colour at the opposite ends of the spectrum may be used to give a balanced scheme. While sensual harmony and composition of form and colour add to a good feng shui interior, colours can also be used to disguise or hide ugly details and badly proportioned walls.

Colours are classified as either yin or yang. Generally, all cool colours (blue, green, white) are yin and all warm colours (red, orange, yellow) yang. The balance of yin and yang, and the use of favourable colours that are based on the Birth Element of the user of the space is an important consideration when designing the interior. As shown in Table 1 on page 25, colours can be classified under the Five Elements:

- green (Wood/east); related to wood whose foliage evokes the energy of potent growth, youthfulness, posterity and harmony with other colours. It is the colour of the dragon of the east;
- red (Fire/south); reflects the yang principle, and is the symbol of virtue and sincerity;
- yellow (Earth/west); emblematic of the earth, yellow denotes the yang principle. The colour is used for geomantic blessings, and charms to ward off evil influences are written on yellow paper;
- white (Gold/west); the symbol of purity and the colour of autumn; and
- black (Water/north); represents yin and it is related to winter. It denotes the consequence of man, death, mourning and penance. In metaphysical terms, it is the colour of calamity, guilt and evil influences.

Shapes and colours spell the nature of things. They are either yin (cool colours and concave) or yang (warm colours and convex). When yin is too strong, it turns to yang. This picture portrays the contrast and intensity of yin and yang colours.

Warm colours can be said to be yang and cool colours yin. The yellow in sunflowers is yang, while the green in the leaves is yin. However, in this painting, green (Wood Element) reinforces red (Fire Element), which in turn enhances yellow (Earth Element).

Earth Element. Here, Earth is indicated by the yellow squares. It is in harmony with the red squares.

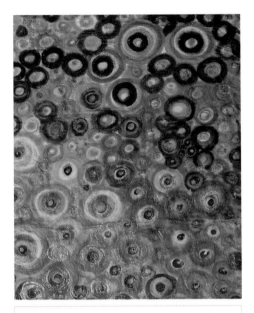

In this picture, the Water Element is represented by the colour black, and the Gold by white and the circular patterns. This shows the harmony of Water and Gold Elements.

Here, the Wood Element is expressed in the elongated rectangles. The wavy patterns depict the Water Element. This painting is harmonious as Wood and Water complement each other.

The wavy pattern of this painting illustrates the Water Element.

INTEGRATING ARCHITECTURE WITH FENG SHUI

In a world of increasing complexity and advanced technology, assessing the feng shui of a place must not be confined to *Xuanxue* (theories related to the *Yijing*, yin and yang, the Eight Trigrams, and the like). Architectural and structural considerations are equally important. The social and cultural needs of the users must be addressed; the functional and environmental aspects of a building cannot be ignored in the design of the tangible and intangible.

Although geomancers are not architects or interior designers, it is important that they have a basic knowledge of building construction and a good sense of design. Without such knowledge, even if they detect poor feng shui features or poor planning, they will be unable to rectify errors in terms of architectural aesthetics.

A building's external and internal spaces are subject to symbolic representation. For thousands of years symbols have been used in Chinese literature and customs, as well as feng shui, to express people's wishes. Wholesome shapes are good symbols, while unwholesome shapes represent misfortune. Squares (representing the earth), circles (representing the heavens), rectangles and balanced shapes are auspicious. On the other hand, triangles, such as an unstable three-legged chair, L-shape and other unbalanced shapes are inauspicious. If a building or building complex is irregular in shape, adding an element to it can help rectify the imbalance. For example if a house is L-shaped, a tree, a light or a well-designed sculpture can be placed to enhance the sense of balance.

Climatic and geographical conditions, natural light and air movement, sound and thermal levels all affect the feng shui of a building. Climatic conditions dictate temperature, humidity, radiation, speed of wind and rainfall, and consequently, geographical positioning

(below left) The simple depiction of vertical lines in the building expresses the Wood Element; (below right) Circular buildings represent the Gold Element, and it is fortuitous to place such structures next to sources of water.

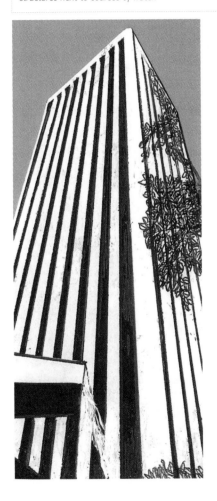

of buildings is closely related to these conditions. Thus in northern China, houses and buildings face south to avoid the bitter north wind. Homes facing north are said to suffer from the ill effects of poor feng shui.

In the tropics where the climate is hot, wet and humid, buildings should be designed to protect inhabitants from the hot sun, heavy rain and dampness from the ground. Buildings with little protection from these elements are poor feng shui structures, and occupants may suffer from excessively yang (hot) environment or from rheumatism. In hot, humid zones, buildings should be oriented north/south with the main door in harmony with the owner's *minggua* (horoscope).

In temperate countries, the sun is a welcomed asset as it brings yang to the yin. In these places, large areas of glass should be used on the south wall to admit warm sunlight. An efficient heating and ventilation system should be provided for good feng shui. If these break down frequently, the health of the occupants will suffer.

COMMERCIAL AND PUBLIC BUILDINGS

Before a building—whether a high-rise office block or hospital or art gallery—is designed and constructed, the entire site and surrounding environment must be explored and studied carefully. The geological nature and the formation of the land, the topographical features and the existing vegetation of the site, as well as the surrounding areas, must be assessed before decisions regarding the type of foundation, structural framework and placement of the structure can be made. Certainly, buildings should not be sited on areas where there is evidence of soil erosion or settlement, moisture or thermal movement.

The structural components of a building must be designed to support the entire load of the building and resist stress. All load-bearing walls and floors must be stable, weatherproof, fire resistant and structurally sound. Most importantly, to avoid looking excessively heavy and oppressive, structural beams must not span too great a distance. Similarly, freestanding columns should be round to avoid affecting the interior with sharp corners that cause *shaqi* (overly vibrant qi).

High-rise buildings in particular affect the built environment as they can be seen from miles away. Height is therefore an important consideration, even though a building's height if often limited by economic factors, soil conditions, and government laws and regulations. Since feng shui is closely related to the financial considerations of a project, the most economical height should be decided upon after careful cost analysis.

The interiors should reflect balance and harmony in terms of design elements, the use of colours, the application of textured materials, and the installation of various mechanical, ventilation and lighting schemes. The doors and entrances, particularly the main door, are very important features and should be suitably designed and placed with due consideration to their ceremonial importance. The main door, the most important element, must be sited with reference to the surrounding exterior and interior environment, the birth date of the owner, the birth date of the building and the overall plan of the building. The design and dimensions of the door must also be built to feng shui requirements.

In addition to ensuring that the building designs and plans conform to feng shui rules, it is important to ensure that proper security devices such as fire alarm systems are installed and there is an efficient means of escape. Artificial plants or ornamental objects should not obstruct passages to fire escape routes or staircases. The distance from the remotest corner of the office to the fire escape should meet with local authority building regulations, but it should not be too near which is uneconomical as there is less working or rentable space, nor too far.

As for toilets, these should not be placed in the north because north is sometimes regarded as a sacred direction. In addition, the entrance to the male and female toilets should not be located too near to each other, and it is good practice to place a store or utility room between the toilets.

The 88-storeyed Petronas Towers in Malaysia are based on geometric forms of interlocking squares (Earth Element) from which triangular (Fire Element) and semi-circular spaces extend to create more usable space. There is unity in the structure because the Earth and Fire Elements in the square and triangular spaces are in harmony with each other.

Commercial buildings

Good planning and good business strategies are important factors for inviting good feng shui. With commercial buildings, a thorough market analysis must be made. The feasibility study of the market analysis, the suitability of the site, the drawing up of an appropriate brief on planning or schedule of accommodation, and the identification of prospective clients are important factors and are all part and parcel of the project's feng shui considerations. In addition, the location of the site, accessibility to the site, location of the main door, ease of movement from one space to the next, planning and design, and the relationship between the commercial project and other nearby complexes are prime factors indicative of a project's success or failure.

The location of the main door of an office or company is a crucial consideration in commercial projects since an auspiciously sited main entrance can bring in success and good fortune. Its location can be assessed and decided by the *Minggua* Method or other methods (see Part Three for an explanation of these methods). It can also be determined by the study of the geographical and environmental factors. In most cases, all factors must be taken into consideration when placing the main entrance. The front door should be designed to carry the spirit of the corporate image; it should made of high quality materials and located in a prominent position. It should not be in alignment with the back door. If it is, a screen or wall should be placed to break the *shaqi*, the excessively vibrant energy which may cause ill health or bad luck. If several doors are built in alignment, a chime should be hung to disperse the congested qi.

Although developers do not necessarily take feng shui considerations into account, potential occupants of an office block or commercial building are becoming increasingly sensitive to feng shui and environmental needs. The intangible aspects of a building can no longer be overlooked. In the case of Foster's 47-storey Hong Kong and Shanghai Bank, the original structure, which presented an inward symbol, was redesigned to give an upward symbol.

An important consideration is that high-rise office blocks must be situated on prominent sites with easy access for people and vehicles, and close to a rapid transit transport system and public facilities such as food and shopping centres. The site should allow for adequate customer parking, loading and unloading service facilities, and an efficient rubbish disposal system. Good planning should facilitate an efficient circulation of people, cross ventilation and the harmonious use of natural and artificial lighting.

Office spaces should be flexible enough to allow for subletting, and it is advantageous to design and build collapsible partitions to accommodate changes in tenancy. The possibility of future extensions must also be taken into account. If the project is a mixed residential and commercial development, there must be functional and physical integration of the different components. Pedestrian routes should be one of the first planning considerations.

The location of the chief executive's office should be chosen with reference to his *minggua*. The room should be relatively spacious and appropriately furnished. The door, desk and chairs should be placed in accordance with feng shui rules, for example, the chair should be placed against a solid wall rather than a glass wall and the desk should ideally face the main door. The lighting, acoustics and ambience of the room should encourage harmonious dialogue. It is the same with the conference room where the person chairing the meeting should be seated in front of a solid wall.

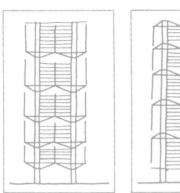

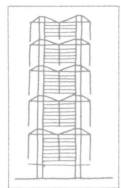

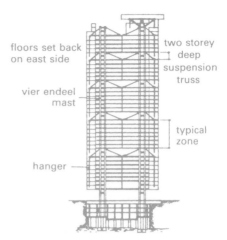

floors set back on east side

two storey deep suspension truss

vier endeel mast

typical zone

hanger

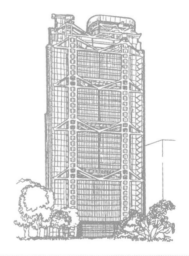

Figure 19 – The sketches above show the original structure of the Hong Kong and Shanghai Bank and the changes that were made to it. True to the dictates of feng shui, the bank (left) sits at the foot of Victoria Park and faces the sea, with the hill behind to protect it and the view in front to enhance its wealth. Still, changes had to be made to the internal structure to improve the building's feng shui.

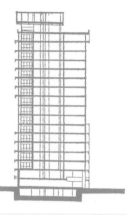

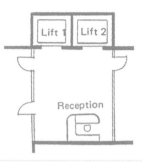

Figure 21 — The drawing shows a spacious office lift lobby with offices on either side. The lobby accommodates a reception area which helps to direct clients and visitors to the various offices in an efficient manner. Company logos and signboards should be placed with reference to the Minggua of the owner and director of the company. Offices should be planned to allow executives to circulate with ease via an interconnecting network. Narrow corridors and the awkward placement of office doors should be avoided.

Figure 20 — This building looks simple in section. However, at 18 storeys high, it could do with more than one level below the ground, and the height of the floors on the lower levels could be more generous. As it is, the qi of the ground level is stifled because the ceiling height is too low.

Figure 22 — In this cross section of a building, the structure is fortuitously sited with the entrance facing the lower ground and the rear portion facing the hill. Efficient drainage is provided by a deep surface drain just below the hill. The foundations are structurally sound and proper tanking has been provided on the retaining wall.

Figure 23 — In this illustration, the rear of the building is sited on the lower ground. The building is triangular, as if half of the word jin (Gold), when rendered in Chinese, has been cut off. This is inauspicious and bodes ill luck.

Public buildings

Public buildings, such as museums, art galleries and hospitals, may not be subjected to the rigours of feng shui assessment as much as commercial buildings. This is because public buildings, being either government or corporate owned, are not sold or leased to business investors and there is less urgency to make substantial profits.

Still, it is important to consider the following: location of site in relation to other buildings; external shape and internal space; structure and cladding; flexibility and feasibility; and lighting and mechanical items. The location of the site should be free from the ill effects of bad feng shui. External shape should be in harmony with the surrounding built forms, and internal space should allow for efficient movement of people. Large public buildings should be sited in accordance with the rules of feng shui; must be easily accessible; must have sufficient parking facilities; and provision must also be made to accommodate future expansion and changes in the feng shui cycle, which changes once every 20 years. Further explanation of the feng shui cycle can be found in Part Three of this book.

In museums and art galleries, freestanding columns should be round because columns with sharp corners create *shaqi*. The cladding should shield the interior from glare without being too reflective. The interior space should allow for flexibility in displaying artworks. Special or artificial lighting may be required to create a suitable ambience as well as enhance the exhibits. Frank Lloyd Wright's Guggenheim Museum in New York, which is based on an interesting continuous smooth-flowing and column-free spatial concept, is a fine example of an art museum of Gold Element.

In shopping centres, circulation routes must be carefully planned so that shops get maximum exposure to the public. Multi-level or double volume spaces within a centre enhance the qi and interest of the interior, and the use of interesting and attractive shops signs can help provide a refreshing atmosphere. Lighting should be designed to complement rather than detract from the shop signs.

In addition, the symbolism of words used in the signs must be auspicious as the following two examples demonstrate: QINGSHUI WOODWORKS, where *qingshui* means 'clear water', which nourishes wood; and DADI GOLDSMITH, where *dadi* means 'huge earth', which produces gold. In contrast, the following examples illustrate the inauspicious symbolism of words: JINJIN WOODWORKS, where *jin* means 'gold', which cuts wood; HUOSHAN GOLDSMITH, where *huo* means 'fire', which melts gold.

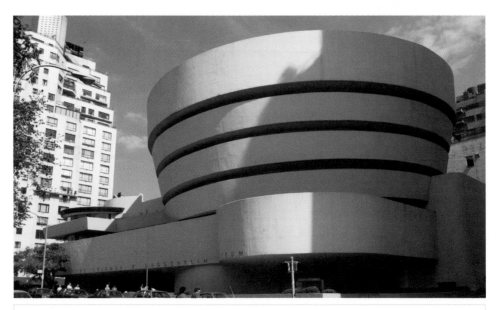

The Guggenheim Museum, opened in October 1959 six months after Wright's death, expresses community and homogenity. Its lack of sharp corners makes it a favourable feng shui structure.

Logos used for company trademarks and signs must also be well conceived. Each shape is associated with an Element. A triangle is Fire; a rectangle, Wood; a circle, Gold; a free-flowing form, Water; and a square, Earth. A logo may be made up of two or more shapes, and one should ensure the shapes are in harmony. For example, a triangle should not be combined with a circle because fire melts gold.

Figure 24 – This symbol would be more balanced if one of the fishes is white.

Figure 27 – This logo is not good because it looks like a cross. To the Chinese, the cross signifies problems unsolved.

Figure 25 – The logo on the left symbolises conflict. The one on the right is better as the upward arrow is balanced by the downward arrow.

Figure 26 – Logos that depict upright arrows are lucky logos.

Figure 28 – Dragons symbolise power, authority and vitality and hence, make good logos.

Where hospitals are concerned, the entrances for patients, visitors, staff and emergency services must be well placed to facilitate efficiency, and the reception area must be immediately apparent. The different areas within a hospital must also be placed appropriately and sensitively. For example, hospital mortuaries (being a yin area) should not be located next to restaurants (yang) or other yang areas, such as pharmacies, where there is heavy human traffic.

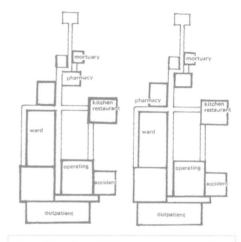

Figure 29 – (above left) This is a poor example of planning which was then changed to create better feng shui; (right) The mortuary, originally sited next to the pharmacy, was shifted to improve feng shui.

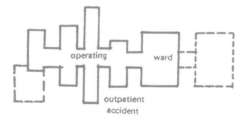

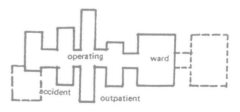

Figure 30 – The original plan (above left) of the hospital had one entrance for outpatients and emergency admissions. Much confusion was created and eventually another entrance (right) was added to ease the pressure of circulation. The change also improved the qi of the entrance.

Religious buildings, such as churches and temples, can also be classified as public buildings. Most Chinese buildings and temples are sited and designed with reference to the feng shui of the site. In Southeast Asia, Chinese temples are based on the concept of balance, symmetry and wall enclosures, and are often oriented with reference to the precepts of geomancy. For example, Thian Hock Keng in Singapore and many other early temples built were orientated with the front facing the sea to capture *shengqi* (vibrant energy) and the rear facing a hilly site or higher ground.

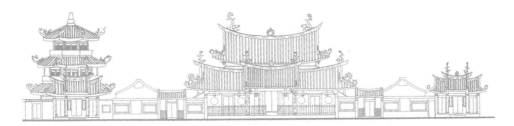

(above) Sketch of Thian Hock Keng temple in Telok Ayer Street, Singapore. In the early colonial days, the sea extended inland to as far as Telok Ayer Street. In 1819, a joss-house for the Goddess of the Sea was built above the foreshore for the Chinese to give their thanks for a safe journey as they arrived on junks. By 1840, the main structure of the temple was completed. The photograph of the temple (right) was taken in the late 70s.

RESIDENTIAL BUILDINGS

Some feng shui practices are a result of old habits. For example, it appears that during ancient times, the amount of taxes on houses was determined by the width and frontage of the building. Residents succeeded in paying less tax by making their homes as narrow as they possibly could. Since then, it was thought that a narrow frontage brought 'luck' to the residents. Despite the intricacies of feng shui and its complicated system of computation known only to experts, some general practices for the siting of homes originated out of practical reasons. Here are some of the standard principles.

Location

Homes should be constructed on high ground and not in valleys. Surely this is a practical suggestion as low-lying areas may be prone to flooding. Homes should not stand on the triangular lot at a 'Y' junction. This sounds rather severe and unreasonable, but it is a fact that vehicles are more prone to accidents at such junctions. Moreover, a triangular lot is difficult to handle in terms of landscaping and planning the site.

Homes should not be sited at the end of narrow streets or lanes. This sounds illogical or superstitious, but such dwellings are seen to be 'unfortunate'. Perhaps from past experience, it was found that homes in such locations were inaccessible in times of danger, for instance during an outbreak of fire, where tenants might have difficulty getting out of the narrow lane to get help. However, it does not mean that homes situated on the main road will receive good luck and health. In tropical countries, it is a practical arrangement when the western wall/walls can be built solid to give privacy and as well to shade the home from the hot setting sun. Appendix 1 and 2 shows

The ideal feng shui is shown in this painting by the author. The houses are sited on a 'horseshoe' fertile site bounded by the Azure Dragon of the yang mountainous range on the left, the White Tiger of the yin hilly site on the right and the lofty mountain at the back (north), which protects the site from evil influences. On the south, a calm meandering stream flows by. It is believed that blessings are transmitted from the north to the south as good cosmic breath comes down the slope this way.

more examples of the auspicious and inauspicious siting of homes and their effects on the feng shui of the occupants (these examples are based on information taken from the *Imperial Encyclopedia* and the *Water Dragon Classics* of AD 600).

Gardens and trees

In China, the southwesterly winds that blow during summer are most refreshing. It is therefore not surprising that geomancer's insist on having a vacant lot to the south for

It is unfortunate to have one's home oriented south of a graveyard as the occupants of the home would be disturbed by evil forces.

Trees planted near the front gate spell evil influences. Also, fast growing trees should not be planted in courtyards as they may be attacked by evil forces.

good fortune. As the sun is hottest at the west, this arrangement can be looked upon as practical. The southern side is thus ideal for an open field or garden.

Trees on the northwest of the site are said to play a protective role and bring happiness to the family. However, very few people are able to explain the logic or the origin behind this belief. Perhaps it originated from the common practice of planting big trees in the northwest of China to shelter dwellings from the yellow dust that was periodically carried by the northwesterly winds that blew from the Gobi Desert.

Watercourses should be seen and harsh looking rocky formations should be camouflaged by feng shui trees.

House at a 'Y' junction. Occupants of homes sited at 'Y' junctions may suffer from fright or misfortune.

On the other hand, trees are not always seen to be 'protective' towards the household and are sometimes believed to obstruct the 'entry of wealth'. For example, a big tree planted in front of the main door cuts out much welcomed sunshine for the house and its occupants.

The interior

In feng shui, the most important part of a building should be located centrally. In a house, this would be the living room, which is indeed the hub and focal point for the family. This is a practical arrangement as a centrally located living area is easily accessible for members of the family.

Every space or room in a house should be of an appropriate size or scale in accordance with its importance. The living room should be larger than the dining room. Similarly, the master bedroom should be larger than the guest room. Even the number of bedrooms in a house is said to affect the feng shui. A house with one, two, five, six, seven or nine bedrooms is considered good but one with three, four or eight bedrooms symbolises ill fortune.

The location of the rooms is also important, and here the theory of the Five Elements is applied. Very often the feng shui expert insists that the kitchen should face either east or south so as not to upset the orders of nature. Wood is related to the east, while fire is related to the south. Therefore, to orientate the kitchen towards a direction related to wood or fire is surely a good practice. In another example, bedrooms should not be placed next to the kitchen. This sounds superstitious but it is a practical point to consider. After all, the bedroom would receive cooking fumes and fires often start from the kitchen.

Kitchens must be designed in a practical working triangle. The cooking area is one feature that requires careful placement. We are, after all, what we eat! It is therefore important to place the stove in an area of *shengqi* (vibrant energy). This area is one that has a plentiful supply of fresh air—to prevent the build-up of noxious gases—and should also be free from obstruction to allow ease of movement. Most geomancers prefer to place the stove with reference to the user's year of birth. The theory of yin and yang also applies to where wells or sources of water supply are placed. Water is yin and fire from the stove is yang. Yin and yang are of opposite principles, and to place a stove next to a water source is unwise as calamity might befall the people.

Another important consideration is the back door. Houses must have a back door; a house without one spells death and misfortune. This appears irrational but the absence of a back exit certainly causes inconvenience to the housewife (or anyone in particular) who has to have access to the backyard. It is equally important that the back door must not be in line with the main front entrance. If the back and front doors are in line, fortune that enters the home will escape through the back.

Where we place our electronic and electrical appliances, such as computers and televisions, must also be considered carefully as they emit energy and noise; if they malfunction, they can also

N
▲

Figure 31 – The example above illustrates the defect of shaqi through the front and back doors. When both doors are in alignment, the qi passes through too quickly and adversely affects the luck of the tenants. In this case, the owner lost a great deal of money. To rectify, the entrance was simply redesigned by placing a screen in front of the main door. Where possible, renovation work can be done to relocate one of the doors.

be sources of pollution. All man-made equipment with the potential to cause ill health is considered poor feng shui. Place such equipment and electronic devices in areas where they are not used for resting, eating and relaxing.

The following drawings of house plans illustrate some of the main feng shui defects and how they were rectified.

Figure 32 – This house has several feng shui defects. The second bedroom, which is occupied by a person of Water Element, is located too near the kitchen (Fire Element) for comfort. Ventilation in the bedroom is also poor as air only comes in through the window at the end of the corridor. In addition, the dining room is too far from the kitchen and the living room faces the setting sun.

Figure 33 – This house has its entrance set back to the south. Even though the approach to the living space is pleasant, the living room is too narrow which restricts the flow of qi. The kitchen is poorly lit and is therefore too yin. The bathroom is in the north, which is not a desirable location. To improve the feng shui, the main entrance is pushed out to make a more spacious entrance, allowing qi to flow in. The living room is also enlarged to allow qi to flow easily. The kitchen is enlarged to allow more natural light and ventilation.

Figure 34 – In this plan, the entrance to the house is set back in a tight space. The kitchen is small and dining space, limited. In addition, the kitchen and part of the dining space are covered by a lean-to roof that appears awkward. Irrespective of the owner's Minggua, this house plan needs to be changed to improve the feng shui. The house was thus lengthened, the kitchen and dining areas shifted to the east, and the entrance pushed out to make the house more wholesome with all the spaces under one roof.

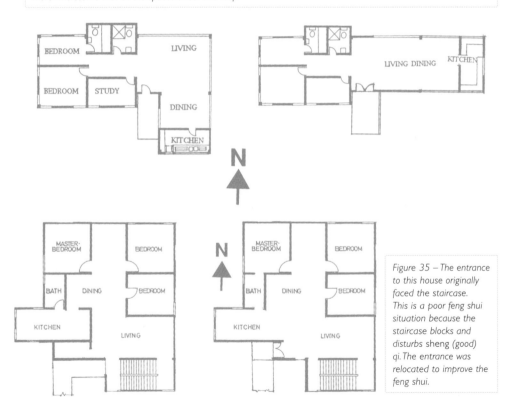

Figure 35 – The entrance to this house originally faced the staircase. This is a poor feng shui situation because the staircase blocks and disturbs sheng (good) qi. The entrance was relocated to improve the feng shui.

Figure 36 – The east-facing entrance of this house was not suitable for the owner, whose horosocope is Zhengua, which required a south-facing orientation. The location of the storeroom spoilt the spatial quality of the living/dining space. To rectify the defects, the entrance was moved to the south and the storeroom was demolished to enlarge the living/dining and kitchen areas.

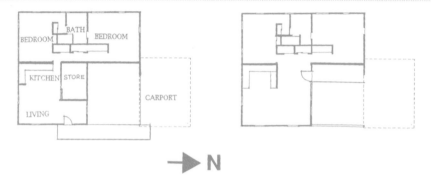

Figure 37 – Symbolism plays an important role in feng shui. The plan shows a house shaped like the word kou *(mouth), symbolising posterity. However, the feng shui was affected by the tree planted in the central courtyard, which rendered the symbol* kun *(difficult). The tree was duly removed. Trees with wide spreading roots should not be planted in a small courtyard.*

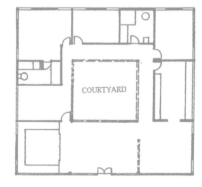

MYTHICAL ORIGINS OF SOME FENG SHUI PRECEPTS

Admittedly not all practices in feng shui arose out of practical reasons. Some emerged from ancient theories of mysticism while others emerged from superstition. Here are some of them.

The doors of the devil

An old legend reveals that in ancient times there grew on Mount Du Su in the northeastern sea, a huge blossom tree which covered an area of a few thousand square miles. The lowest branches inclined towards the northeast and all those who went near the tree were devoured by demons. The evil spirits were later conquered by the good spirits Shen Shu and Yu Lei. Since then people have painted the portraits of these good spirits on their main doors to ward off evil influences, hence these spirits are also called door gods. It has since become essential for temples to have the door gods painted on their front doors.

This superstitious belief spread to as far as Japan. At the Imperial Palace, temples and pagodas were constructed at the northeastern part to block evil spirits.

Door gods of the Wak Hai Cheng Bio temple in Singapore

Therefore, the northeast is said to be 'the door of the devil' and the southwest, the 'back door of the devil'. Should doors be made along these directions, bad luck and ill health would befall the occupants of the house. If a building is orientated along the 'door of the devil', its doors must be relocated or designed at an oblique angle to avoid calamity and evil spirits.

One would become a king is one's home is orientated towards the south

Contrary to belief surrounding the northeast, the south is reputed to be of good orientation. There is an old saying in Chinese: *chao nan er chen wang* (if one is orientated towards the south one would become a king). This appears to be utterly optimistic, but in the tropical regions orientating one's dwelling towards the south is certainly a wise idea as it does not get the full impact of the hot setting afternoon sun.

Good qi always descends from slopes, and from north to south. Not only should the south be vacant to benefit from the yang qi, the other three sides must be 'closed' to accumulate the good influences. A hill on the northern side is ideal as it protects the site from malignant implications. It is even better when the south slopes down to a river or a sea. Many temples in Singapore were planned in such a manner during the early 19th century.

The White Tiger and the Azure Dragon

These mythical guardians of good report and protection are symbolised by the White Tiger of the west (or right) and the Azure Dragon of the east (or left). Often found in traditional Chinese temple design, the White Tiger is always placed on the right side of a building and the Azure Dragon on the left. They can also be represented by the words *hu xiao* (tiger roars) on the right and *loong yin* (dragon speaks) on the left.

Legend has it that the White Tiger was the son of a courtier of the tyrant Chou Wang of the Yuan dynasty. The courtier was murdered by Chou Wang's aides. In trying to avenge his father's murder, the son was killed. He was later canonised as the spirit of the White Tiger star. The Azure Dragon was one of the chief generals of the last emperor of the Yuan dynasty. He was made a prisoner of war, executed and later deified as the Azure Dragon star.

Yin and yang are sometimes identified with the Azure Dragon and the White Tiger respectively. The picture, found in the main prayer hall of the Leong San See temple in Singapore, depicts the dragon.

Part Three

The Method School of Assessing Feng Shui

There are several ways of assessing the feng shui of a building—some based on method and calculation (the Method School), others through studying landforms, detecting watercourses and locating important areas in the qi points (the Form School). The modern feng shui practitioner makes use of all available knowledge and examines the building with reference to every method with which he is familiar. Here, the Method School is described in more detail.

One approach in the application of the Method School is based on the Eight Characters of Birth; these characters are paired and are known as the Four Pillars of Destiny. One's destiny is based on the predominant Element of Birth, which in turn is based on the Stem of the day of birth. The Element of Birth could be Wood, Fire, Earth, Gold or Water. The Season of Birth and the other Branches and Stems of Birth together will help to determine whether the Birth Element is strong or weak. More information on the Element of Birth is presented in *Personalise Your Feng Shui And Transform Your Life*.

If an assessment is to be made of an existing building, the feng shui practitioner will examine the site and study the relationship of the existing structure with its surrounding physical and built environment, as well as the topography of the land, noting the favourable and unfavourable features. In addition, he may analyse the owner's *minggua* (horoscope, where one's destiny is based on the *gua* (Trigram) that one is associated with) and his Year of Birth. Every year is associated with a Trigram (see Appendix 3). Knowing one's year of birth and striving to ensure that the surrounding environment is compatible with it will help bring harmony and good fortune.

When the site has been studied, the geomancer sketches a diagram of the location and determines the favourable positions for placing the important areas, such as the main door, master bedroom, kitchen or living area. He also checks the existing building or the plans for the proposed building and makes his recommendations.

However, determining the favourable locations is only one aspect of the assessment. The other equally important factors to consider are the *yun* (era) during which the structure was built or will be built, the topography of the site, the landscape and other physical features that may be present. All these are best analysed by skilled practitioners; the more skilful they are in terms of site planning and design, the better the feng shui. For complicated building complexes, the best geomancers are those also trained in architectural design or engineering.

This section presents an explanation of three of the approaches within the Method School, namely the *Minggua* Method, the *Bazhai Mingjin* Method and the *Feixing* Method. All these approaches are based on the *minggua* of the users or owners for the orientation of the building.

THE *MINGGUA* (HOROSCOPE) METHOD

In the *Minggua* Method, the locations of the important areas are determined by the compatibility of the Element of the *gua* with the direction or location of the building. The table below shows the relationship between the Trigrams, the Five Elements Elements and the Eight Directions.

For example, the east direction (*zhen* of Wood Element) is good for the *kangua* (*kan* Trigram), which is north and of Water Element. The southwest direction (*kun* of Earth) is compatible for the *qiangua* (*qian* Trigram), which is northwest and Gold, and the *duigua* (*dui* Trigram), which is west and Gold. The east (*zhen* of Wood) and southeast (*xun* of Wood) directions are in harmony with the *ligua* (*li* Trigram), which is south and Fire. The north direction (*kan* of Water) is good for the Zhengua (*zheng* Trigram), which is

Table 7 Relationship between Trigrams, Elements and the Directions

Trigram	Element	Direction
qian	Gold	northwest (signifies the heavens and masculinity)
kun	Earth	southwest (represents the earth and femininity)
zhen	Wood	east (indicates change)
kan	Water	north (indicates danger)
gen	Earth	northeast (refers to the mountains)
xun	Wood	southeast (refers to the wind)
li	Fire	south (associated with the sun, lightning and fire)
dui	Water / Gold	west (signifies the clouds and moisture)

east and Wood and the *Xungua* (*xun* Trigram), which is southeast and Wood. The south is auspicious for the *Gengua* (*gen* Trigram), which is northeast and Earth.

In contrast, the southwest is not good for the *kangua* (north and Water). The northwest or the west is not auspicious for the *zhengua* (east and Wood) or the *xungua* (southeast and Wood). The south is not in harmony with the *qiangua* (northwest and Gold) or the *duigua* (west and Gold). The east or the southeast is not compatible with the *gengua* (northeast and Earth) or the *kungua* (southwest and Earth). The northwest is not good for the *ligua* (south and Fire).

The compatibility and incompatibility of the Trigrams with the directions may be summarised in Table 8. However, a detailed assessment of feng shui requires a more comprehensive analysis of the horoscope of the occupants of the buildings and a complete analysis of the site and its surroundings.

Table 8 Compatibility of the Trigrams with the directions

Gua and Element	Favourable directions	Unfavourable directions
qiangua of Gold Element	SW, W, NW	N, E, SE, S
kungua of Earth Element	W, NW, NE	N, E, SE
zhengua of Wood Element	SE, S, N, E	SW, W, NW
kangua of Water Element	NE, W, NW	SW, SE, N
gengua of Earth Element	SW, W, NW	N, E, SE
xungua of Wood Element	E, SE, N	SW, W, NW
ligua of Fire Element	SE, S, E	SW, W, NW
duigua of Gold Element	NW, W, NE	N, E, SE, S

THE *BAZHAI MINGJIN* (FOUR HOUSES) METHOD

The *Bazhai Mingjin* Method or Four Houses Method is fairly similar to the *Minggua* Method in that it is based on the year of birth and its related Trigram. In this method, people may be broadly classified into either the Eastern Four Houses or the Western Four Houses according to their natal Trigram or their year of birth. People with *minggua* of *li, kan, zhen* and *xun* fall under the Eastern Four Houses. Those with *minggua* of *qian, kun, gen* and *dui* come under the Western Four Houses.

The *gua* of the Eastern Four Houses of *li, kan, zhen* and *xun* are grouped together and between them, *zhen* and *xun*, both of Wood Element, produce *li* (Fire Element); *kan* (Water Element) produces *zhen* and *xun*, both of Wood.

Similarly, among the Western Four Houses, *qian* and *dui* are both Gold, and *gen* and *kun* are Earth. Earth produces Gold, and thus Earth and Gold are productive Elements. Those who belong to the Eastern Houses should not have the entrances to their homes, bedrooms or kitchens positioned in the westerly directions. Similarly, those of the Western Houses should not have entrances, bedrooms and kitchens in the easterly directions.

To locate the living or working spaces, the centre of the building has to be determined. This is easily done if the shape of the building is a square or a rectangle. However, if the shape is awkward, the centre of the building has to be worked out. A measured drawing has to be undertaken if plans of the building are not available.

The natal charts or horoscopes of the users of the building are not the only guidelines for the assessment of the feng shui of a place. The topographic features and levels, together with the man-made and natural elements around the site, have to be assessed. For example, even though it is generally auspicious to have a hill or high ground at the back of the building, if the owner of the building is of the Water Element and the hill is of Fire shape, the hill does not enhance the site. It must be noted that man-made elements can be classified under the Five Elements, and the theory of the compatibility or destructibility of the Elements also applies in assessing the surrounding landscape.

THE *FEIXING* (FLYING STAR) METHOD

The most popular method for assessing the feng shui of a place is the *Feixing* or Flying Star Method. This method reveals the auspicious and inauspicious influences on a building during various *yun* (age or era).

In the feng shui cycle, each era lasts 20 years, and there are nine 20-year cycles that repeat themselves. Using the variation of numbers from 1 to 9 and by equating the numbers with the Five Elements, the auspiciousness or inauspiciousness of a place is assessed according to the portents of the era the building was constructed. Table 9 shows the numbers that are equated with various eras and their corresponding Elements. So a building constructed in 1985 is considered to be in *yun* 7. It is also considered to be in the *xiayuan* (lower *yuan*), as the nine eras are divided into three *yuan* (tiers), namely the *shangyuan* (upper *yuan*), the *zhongyuan* (middle *yuan*) and the *xiayuan* (lower yuan). This means that during the era of *qiyun* (seven), the magic number 7 is most auspicious.

In the *Feixing* Method, Magic Diagrams are an important tool that feng shui experts rely on. Magic Diagrams reveal the changes in feng shui cycles every 20 years and have their roots in the *Luoshu* diagram. According to legend, the first emperor of the Xia

Table 9 The eras and their Elements

Yun (era) numbers	Element	Years	Yuan (tier)
1	Water	1864 – 1883	shangyuan (upper)
2	Earth	1884 – 1903	
3	Wood	1904 - 1923	
4	Wood	1924 – 1943	zhongyuan (middle)
5	Earth	1944 – 1963	
6	Gold	1964 – 1983	
7	Gold	1984 – 2003	xiayuan (lower)
8	Earth	2004 – 2023	
9	Fire	2023 - 2043	

dynasty (2140–1711 BC), by the name of Dayu, saw black (yin) and white (yang) dots on the back of a huge tortoise when he was building outlets to discharge the flood waters of the Huang He. A diagram of these dots was made and named the *Hetu.* During the Zhou dynasty (1231–1135 BC), the dots on the Hetu were translated into Trigrams. When the dots and the Trigrams were drawn to relate to the Eight Directions and the Five Elements, a diagram called the *Luoshu Tu* (the drawings of the book of Luo) was formed.

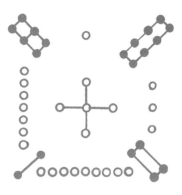

Figure 38 – The Luoshu Tu

The *Luoshu Tu* diagram illustrates the yang (odd/white) numbers 1, 3, 5, 7 and 9, which are associated with the heavens, and the yin (even/black) numbers 2, 4, 6 and 8, which are related to the earth. This particular diagram is based on *yun* 5, as can be seen from the five dots in the centre. South, being of Fire Element, is the most extreme yang element associated with the number 9 and has been used in the design of imperial palaces since ancient times. It is from this diagram that base divination plates (below) were devised for the purpose of divining the next era. The *Luoshu Tu* diagram also forms the basis of the Magic Diagram with its nine squares.

Base Divination Plates

Water Star plates (left)

Southeast			South			Southwest		
3	8	1	8	4	6	1	6	8
2	4	6	7	9	2	9	2	4
7	9	5	3	5	1	5	7	3
4	8	6	4	9	2	8	3	1
5	3	1	3	5	7	9	7	5
9	7	2	8	1	6	4	2	6
7	3	5	2	6	4	7	2	9
6	8	1	3	1	8	8	6	4
2	4	9	7	5	9	3	1	5
Northeast			North			Northwest		

(East at left, West at right)

Mountain Star plates (right)

Southeast			South			Southwest		
3	8	1	8	4	6	1	6	8
2	4	6	7	9	2	9	2	4
7	9	5	3	5	1	5	7	3
2	7	9	4	9	2	6	2	4
1	3	5	3	5	7	5	7	9
6	8	4	8	1	6	1	3	8
7	3	5	9	5	7	5	1	3
6	8	1	8	1	3	4	6	8
2	4	9	4	6	2	9	2	7
Northeast			North			Northwest		

(East at left, West at right)

Figure 39 – The Water Star plates (above left, for the front of buildings) and the Mountain Star plates (right, for the back of buildings). Putting the north point pointing downwards, and at the bottom of the divination plates, is a typical Chinese practice. The origin of this could be due to feng shui reasoning where north is not as auspicious as the south.

To assess the feng shui of an existing building, the geomancer must first study the structure's birth chart and orientation, and draw up the divination plates based on his findings. The front of the building refers to the Water Star, while the rear refers to the Mountain Star. Thus, the Water Star plates apply to the front of the building, while the Mountain Star plates apply to the rear of the building. The Water Star tells of the acquisition of wealth and is an indicator of prosperity, while the Mountain Star tells of the state of health of the occupant.

Take an example of a building constructed during the 7th *yun*. If the front of the building faces north, the Water Star Magic Diagram is taken from the plate with 3 its centre (Figure 40). The Mountain Star Magic Diagram of the building is taken from the plate with 2 at its centre (Figure 41). By combining the divination plates and the two diagrams, the final Magic Diagram depicting the auspiciousness of the building can be drawn (Figure 42 overleaf).

South

4	8	6
5	3	1
9	7	2

North

Figure 40 – The Water Star Magic Diagram

South

1	6	8
9	2	4
5	7	3

North

Figure 41 – The Mountain Star Magic Diagram

In the final Magic Diagram, the small numbers in the top left and right corners of each square are assessed in terms of the compatibility of their Elements. The top right numbers indicate the health and personal wellbeing of the occupants (from the Water Star diagram), while those on the top left indicate wealth and prosperity (from the Mountain Star diagram). For the yun of 7, the number 7 indicates immediate 'happening' and the number 8, the next 20-year period. This means that numbers 6, 5, 4, 3, 2 and 1 are distant in the future.

South

1 4|6 **6**	8|8 **2**	6 **4**
9 5|2 **5**	3|4 **7**	1 **9**
5 9|7 **1**	7|3 **3**	2 **8**

North

Figure 42 – The final Magic Diagram

In analysing the compatibility of the Elements, the time frames in feng shui are also considered. For example, in the square 6 of the final Magic Diagram (Figure 42), the top left and right numbers are 1 and 4 respectively. However, they are quite distant from the number 7, which means that both good health and prosperity are quite difficult to obtain. However, the square 3 is auspicious as both the top left and right numbers are 7, the number of the present era.

In analysing the auspiciousness of any part of the house, the diagrams of the productivity and destructibility of the Elements must be considered. For example, the top row of three squares of the final Magic Diagram are auspicious for the following reasons: 1 (Water) + 4 (Wood) is auspicious because Water gives birth to Wood; 6 (Gold) + 8 (Earth) or 8 (Earth) + 6 (Gold) are not inauspicious nor particularly auspicious. Generally, numbers 1, 6 and 8 are considered good although it depends on the other Elements with which they are matched. The numbers 2 and 5 are considered inauspicious while numbers 3, 4, 7 and 9 may be auspicious depending on how they are paired.

As can be seen, the Chinese have used numbers for thousands of years, not only to count but also in fortune telling, to predict the future and to interpret the forces of nature. Numbers are believed to represent the nine stars, which symbolise the essence of the Universe and the Five Elements. Numbers also represent the eight directional orientations coinciding with the eight ancient numerical symbols of the Eight Trigrams.

In summary, all the approaches used in the Method School for the purpose of analysing the feng shui of a building are valid and useful. Each throws light and adds value in the assessment of feng shui. A geomancer can make use of every approach to gather important information relating to the compatibility of the user/owner and the dwelling/building. However, the knowledge gained from the Method School is best combined with the precepts of the Form School. The study of landforms and the location of important areas in the qi points are equally important.

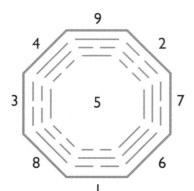

Figure 43 – The numbers and their positions on the Eight Trigrams. Numbers are used to classify the directions, seasons and colours. The numbers 1 and 6 symbolise the North, winter and black; 3 and 8 refer to the East, spring and blue; 2 and 7 the South, summer and red; 4 and 9 the West, autumn and white. The number 5 represents the central position and the colour yellow.

Part Four

Case Studies

The practice of feng shui requires one to learn to live within the natural environment, to respect the forces in nature and to study existing examples of both good as well as not so good feng shui models. By doing so one gains a better understanding of the right approaches to feng shui design. The design principles of classical feng shui buildings and famous structures, both ancient and new, enable one to understand the roots of civilisation and culture of a people.

FENG SHUI IN TRADITIONAL CHINESE BUILDINGS

The examples in this section show the relationship between traditional design concepts and the philosophy of feng shui. In my companion book, *Feng Shui For Success In Business*, you will read that many ancient Chinese cities were sited and planned with reference to feng shui precepts, and any changes in the placement of major or capital cities were made because of changes in the feng shui cycles.

Beijing, the capital city of China, provides a vivid example of a city planned according to the precepts of feng shui. Undoubtedly, many of the classical buildings and religious structures erected during the Ming and Qing dynasties in the city itself were built in accordance with the practice of feng shui. For a more comprehensive account of classical Chinese architecture in and around Beijing, see *Feng Shui In Chinese Architecture*.

Gugong—The Forbidden City

The Gugong has served 24 emperors since AD 1420. It was first built by the Ming ruler, Yong Le (AD 1403–424) in the seventh lunar month of AD 1406. Located within the inner city of Beijing, the former imperial complex was built within a walled enclosure of 1,005 metres by 758 metres and is surrounded by a moat. Over 100,000 builders and workers were conscripted to build the imperial city which then contained over 9,999 rooms and spaces. When the Gugong was completed, it was named Zi Jincheng (Forbidden City). Ordinary people were not allowed to enter it without permission from the royal household.

The imperial palaces in the Gugong were orientated south because it was considered an auspicious orientation for the emperor as he met the gaze of the heavens. The complex and its three main south-facing palaces—Taihe Dian (the Hall of Supreme Harmony), Zhonghe Dian (the Central Hall of Harmony) and Baohe Dian (the Hall of Protection and Harmony)—were built during the *Wuyun*, the fifth era. The palaces were placed along the central axis of the Forbidden City with the back of each palace protected by a man-made hill of coal.

The feng shui of the palaces can be assessed by looking at the *Feixing* Magic Diagram opposite. The small numbers on the top left and right of each of the larger numbers represent the auspiciousness or inauspiciousness of the Water and Mountain Stars. The numbers on the right (the Mountain Star) portray personal happiness and good health, while those on the left (the Water Star) are indicative of prosperity. In this case, the front of the palaces were sited at square 9, which has the Mountain Star 5. The rear has the number 5 Water Star in square 1.

<table>
<tr><td colspan="6" align="center">South</td></tr>
<tr>
<td>9</td><td>8</td><td>5</td><td>4</td><td>7</td><td>6</td>
</tr>
<tr>
<td colspan="2" align="center">**4**</td><td colspan="2" align="center">**9**</td><td colspan="2" align="center">**2**</td>
</tr>
<tr>
<td>8</td><td>7</td><td>1</td><td>9</td><td>3</td><td>2</td>
</tr>
<tr>
<td colspan="2" align="center">**3**</td><td colspan="2" align="center">**5**</td><td colspan="2" align="center">**7**</td>
</tr>
<tr>
<td>4</td><td>3</td><td>6</td><td>5</td><td>2</td><td>1</td>
</tr>
<tr>
<td colspan="2" align="center">**8**</td><td colspan="2" align="center">**1**</td><td colspan="2" align="center">**6**</td>
</tr>
<tr><td colspan="6" align="center">North</td></tr>
</table>

(above) The approach to the magnificent Taihe Dian is a grand flight of stairs divided by the imperial path, over which the Qing emperor was carried in a sedan chair whenever he entered or left the hall. Built in AD 1421, this most impressive building in the Gugong was subjected to two fires and renovated in AD 1669 and 1765; (left) Feixing Magic Diagram of the Forbidden City.

Tiantan—the Temple of Heaven

The temple complex of the Tiantan was a special place of worship during the Ming and Qing dynasties. Located on the southeastern side of Beijing and enclosed by walls, it consists of three main structures: Qi Niandian (the Hall of Prayers for a Good Year), Zhaigong (the Hall of Abstinence) and Huangiu (the Altar of Heaven), all of which were built complete with auspicious feng shui

South

4	8 8	3 6	1
	4	9	2
5	9 3	7 1	5
	3	5	7
9	4 7	2 2	6
	8	1	6

North

symbols, colours and numbers. For example, the open-air platforms that were used by the emperor for worshipping the heavens, the Huanqiu, were built on three concentric rings of terraces paved with marble.

In classical Chinese buildings, as well as feng shui buildings, importance is expressed in the hierarchy of heights and the number of tiers of podiums and roofs. The most important building has three tiers of podiums and three tiers of roofs, and Qi Niandian, being the most important building in the complex of the Tiantan, has a three-tiered roof. The plan and construction details demonstrate the application of significant feng shui symbolism. For example, the concentric rings of marble slabs have been arranged and used as floor finishing materials (visitors standing on these marble slabs will note yang (odd) numbers of marble slabs laid from 9 to 81 on the first ring of the circles).

When the *Feixing* Magic Diagram of the Tiantan was analysed, it was found that there are four approaches to it, but the main approach was perhaps purposely placed in the east so that it had the Water Star 5, and its rear entrance had the Mountain Star 5, since the date of construction was in the fifth *yun* (era) in the feng shui cycle.

(above left) The 38-metre high Qi Niandian stands magnificently on its three-tier white marble podium. The roof apex is capped with a baoding (precious top) portraying celestial power; (above right) Internally, the structure is magnificent. Powerful feng shui and symbolism are expressed in the roof structure and decoration. Circular roofs refer to the heavens and infinity, and cloud motifs symbolise imperial power over the universe. Yang images of dancing golden dragons and phoenix appear in sculptures and paintings on caissons and gold panels.

Yi Heyuan—the Summer Palace

The Yi Heyuan is another excellent example of the feng shui model of imperial palaces. It was designed and built with natural materials, and man-made features were introduced to enhance the feng shui of the place.

The temples in the main complex, comprising the Paiyun Ge and the Fo Xiangge, were constructed on the slope of the Wanshou Shan behind a man-made lake named Kun Minghu. When it was first built in the fifth yun, the *Feixing* Magic Diagram of Fo Xiangge revealed that it was placed at the site with both the Water and Mountain Stars 5. The entrance to the building in the south had the Mountain Star 6, but during the ninth yun in the year 1860, the Water Star changed to 1 (Water Element) and the Mountain Star changed to 9 (Fire Element). The Elements of Fire and Water clashed, and during that year the building complex was razed by foreign troops. In 1891, during the second yun, the *Feixing* Magic Diagram changed and the Water and Mountain Stars at the entrance were 2 and 1 respectively. Ultimately, the complex was rebuilt.

The administration palace of the Yi Heyuan was the Renshou Tang. It was built in 1750 during the fourth yun, and the main entrance to the palace complex was from the east gate. This arrangement was not particularly auspicious, and during the fourth yun the Water and Mountain Stars at the east were 9 and 8 respectively. Both numbers were far from 4 and were thus inauspicious.

One large complex within the Yi Heyuan is the Leshou Tang (the Hall of Happiness in Longevity), built during the fourth yun for the Empress Dowager, Cixi. Its *Feixing* Magic Diagram illustrates that the main entrance connected to the Changlang (Long Gallery) was auspicious. By 1860, the feng shui changed. It was obvious that the stars were inauspicious for that period as the palace was destroyed by foreign forces in the same year.

The timbered Fo Xiangge temple is an ideal example of feng shui principles, with its use of powerful colours and its location overlooking the Kun Minghu in front and hills behind. The temple is built on the highest part of the Wan Shoushan (Longevity Hill) and can be reached by steep stone staircases.

Bishu Shanzhuang in Chengde

About 250 kilometres away from Beijing is Chengde, a historical city lying on the Yan Shan. The Bishu Shanzhuang (which means 'mountain resort in summer') was a very important summer resort for seven out of ten of the Qing rulers. Covering 5,640 square kilometers and containing 384 buildings, its construction was initiated by Emperor Kang Xi in AD 1703 during the fifth *yun*.

Built with auspicious southerly entrances, the structures are sited on good feng shui sites with undulating land, complete with feng shui landscaping—hills, pavilions, crags, woods and ponds—all of which enhance individual buildings and

The feng shui of this summer retreat seems almost perfect because of its scenic beauty and serene environment. There is contrast of yin—lake, stream, valley, shaded areas—and yang—land, hill, sunlit areas. (below left) Built in AD 1703, the walkways of the Jinshan (Gold Hill) are lined with rocks and the view from the top level of the three-tier pavilion is most picturesque; (below right) A closer view of the beautiful timber pagoda and rockery on Jinshan.

the entire built environment. Eight man-made lakes of varying sizes, each dotted with islands, reinforce the qi of the place. Surrounding the resort complex are 12 magnificent temple complexes. These are sited along the foothills east and north of the Bishu Shanzhuang hills, and thus are provided with fortuitous feng shui backing.

FENG SHUI IN WESTERN BUILDINGS

Many classical Renaissance buildings in Europe were surprisingly designed and built with good feng shui orientations. When assessed with reference to feng shui, very often they were found to be fortuitous with regard to the cycle in which they were built. However, it was found that any changes to the *yun* affected the feng shui of the buildings. Figures 44 to 49 describe some examples.

Figure 44 – The plan of the Whitehall Palace, London (1621) can be studied and a Feixing Magic *Diagram (below) drawn with reference to the era of construction, location and orientation. It can be seen that the grand entrance to this Renaissance-building complex, designed by Inigo Jones, was well placed.*

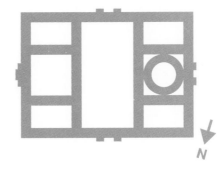

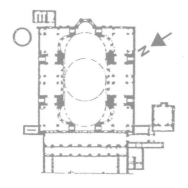

South

4 ⁸ 5	9 ³ 1	2 ¹ 3
3 ⁹ 4	5 ⁷ 6	7 ⁵ 8
8 ⁴ 9	1 ² 2	6 ⁶ 7

North

Figure 45 – The sketch plan above is of the Hagia Sophia in Constantinople, built by Justinian as a Christian church in AD 537. Constructed during the sixth yun, its Feixing Magic Diagram shows that the entrance was well placed as it had the auspicious Water and Mountain Star 6. However, in 1453, its Magic Diagram changed to the seventh cycle. Its entrance could not benefit from the lucky number 7 and it consequently fell under the control of the Saracenic.

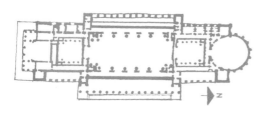

South

3 ⁴ 7	8 ⁸ 3	1 ⁶ 5
2 ⁵ 6	4 ³ 8	6 ¹ 1
7 ⁹ 2	9 ⁷ 4	5 ² 9

North

Figure 46 – Above is a sketch plan of the Elmees St George's Hall in Liverpool, England. The structure was built during the eighth yun. From the Feixing Magic Diagram, it can be seen that the south entrance was attributed with the Water Star 8 for prosperity.

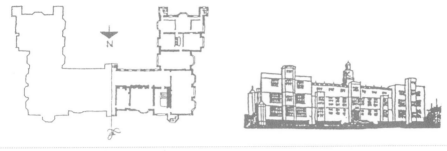

Figure 47 – Hatfield House, Hertfordshire, England, was built in 1611 during the sixth yun. The E-shaped plan had two symmetrical wings. The entrance was suitably placed towards the auspicious south, with Water Star 6 for prosperity and Mountain Star 6 for good health.

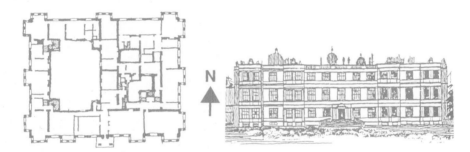

Figure 48 – The main entrance of Longleat House, Wiltshire, England, built in 1580 during the fourth yun, was sited to ensure the occupants' good health. The plan has harmonious balance and is symmetrical in layout.

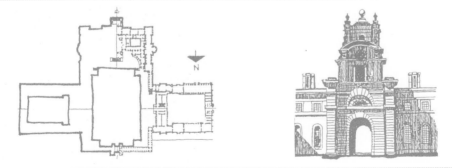

Figure 49 – Blenheim Palace, Oxfordshire, England, was designed by Sir John Vanbrugh in 1705 during the second yun. Its north entrance enjoyed the prosperity of Water Star 2. Its plan was designed on an axial line with perfect balance.

Parisian buildings

The French capital, Paris, is dotted with many innovative buildings that have added vigour and power to the cityscape. Of the many historical buildings and urban structures, the Arc de Triomphe, the Eiffel Tower, the Louvre, the Hùtel des Invalides and Notre Dame Cathedral still bear the greatest symbolic and monumental significance, and remain the main tourist attractions. But Paris is also abuzz with modern innovative buildings such as the commercial centre at La Dèfense and the Pompidou Centre, which are themselves a big draw for architects, scholars and others from all over the world.

The historical monument, the Arc de Triomphe, built in 1806 by Chalgrin, is sited on Paris' central axis of straight roads stretching seven kilometres in length. This main circulation artery connects the Louvre, the Champs Elysèes, Rue de Rivoli, La Dèfense and many other

The Eiffel Tower is of Fire Element and is charged with vibrant energy.

The Grande Arche, Paris

important buildings. These buildings and structures are powerful icons in Paris. The Eiffel Tower, constructed in 1889 for the Paris Exhibition, was designed by bridge builder Alexandre-Gustave Eiffel. Consisting of four bridge-like structural pylons, it reaches over 300 metres high and can be seen from miles around. The tower is of Fire Element and it could influence buildings of Gold or Water Elements. Fortunately, it is far from such buildings.

The most impressive of Parisian modern structures is perhaps the Grande Arche at La Dèfense, a hollowed monolithic U-shaped structure built on a raised podium. The visitor is overwhelmed by the grandeur and monumentality of structure and space as he walks up the countless steps to approach the exhibition rooms on the base level. This modern structure recalls the grandeur and feng shui of the imperial palaces of the Qing dynasty, especially in its monumental approach and symmetrical layout. Countless other multi-storeyed modern buildings have been constructed on the sides of the axis of the Grande Arche. Magnificently landscaped areas, panels for the display of art work and decorative shops offer the visitors an extraordinary focus and sense of symmetrical space.

As described in Part Two, the shape and form of a building determines its Element, and the building's auspiciousness is in turn influenced by the compatibility of that Element with another shape or form that the building might be paired with. Generally, a square (Earth Element) is compatible with a round form (Gold); a triangle (Fire) with a square; a round form with an intuitive form (Water); and a rectangle (Wood) with a triangle.

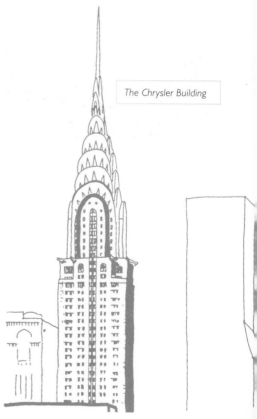

The Chrysler Building

In addition, similar geometrical forms are compatible with each other. For example, New York's Chrysler Building is crowned with Art Deco steel motifs of Gold and Fire Elements. This is neutralised by its squarish plan, creating an overall auspicious pattern of Gold, Earth and Fire.

FENG SHUI AND THE BURIAL GROUND

In ancient China, the wealthy consulted the services of geomancers when there was a death in the family. In Chinese belief, the deceased are associated with yin. When a living being leaves the yang world, 70 per cent of his soul travels to the celestial world while the remainder dwells in the tomb. How well the deceased are buried affects their living descendants. The tomb, therefore, must have auspicious feng shui to benefit the surviving relatives.

It is not surprising therefore that the burial rites of the rich and powerful were carried out with great pomp and ceremony. Of utmost importance was the choice of burial sites, which were carefully assessed by geomancers. It was believed that the *lingpo* (spiritual energy) of the forefathers was linked to those of the descendants. If the forefathers were buried in auspicious feng shui sites, the surviving relatives would enjoy good health and prosperity. Numerous emperors, such as Qin Shi Huang, ordered their mausoleums to be constructed soon after they ascended the throne. Emperor Qin's tomb was designed to express the cosmic order of the heavens and the supreme power he held during his lifetime.

Landscape features, such as hills and lakes, are auspicious and enhance the feng shui of the burial ground. However, the relationship of the landscape with the burial ground has to be assessed before the feng shui of the place can be determined. Some of the essential features that influence the auspice of the burial ground include: *zhushan* (the rear hills at a distance); *shao zhushan* (the hills in front of the distant hills); *qinglong* (the high ground on the left of the burial place); *baihu* (the high ground on the right of the place); high ground around the place; the flow of water from the hills or elsewhere; the qi or energy of the place, and the actual burial site.

The auspiciousness of the features is determined by the degree of harmony established between the different features, the profile of the hills, the balance achieved in terms of the Elements of the features and the quality of the qi of the site. Ideally, the *qinlong* (Azure Dragon) and the *baihu* (White Tiger) should form a pair of hills and meet at the burial ground site in the form of a horseshoe. The Elements of the hills are spelt out by their profiles and shapes: Gold is rounded; Wood, elongated; Water, irregular; Fire, pointed or triangular, and Earth, squarish. The directions or orientations of the hills should be associated with the following compatible Elements: west with Gold; east with Wood; north with Water; south with Fire; and centre with Earth.

The sites of the Ming tombs, grouped on Tianshoushan on the outskirts of Beijing, were chosen because they were surrounded by mountains and also their south side faced low land. Such criteria fulfilled the feng shui requirement of having the Black Turtle (high land) at the rear, the Azure Dragon on the left, the White Tiger to the right and the Red Bird (south) in front. The Qing emperors adopted the Ming culture and practice of feng shui, selecting their burial sites with the help of geomancers. The sketches opposite

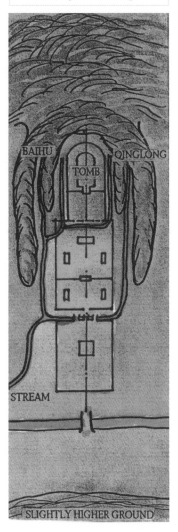

The Ideal feng shui of burial grounds

BAIHU

QINGLONG

TOMB

STREAM

SLIGHTLY HIGHER GROUND

are aerial views of the eastern and western tombs of the Qing emperors, which were built like those of the Ming rulers

The ancient saying *jidi buke wushui* (auspicious ground cannot be one without water) stresses the importance of water features. Another saying, *shanshui xiangjiao, yin yang yong yi* (the hills and the water unite and the yin and yang are in harmony), reinforces the importance of the union and harmony of the hills and water to augur auspicious feng shui. The best feng shui burial ground has to be *tuhou shuisheng, beifeng beishui* (let the crest of the earth be thick and free from rain and flood).

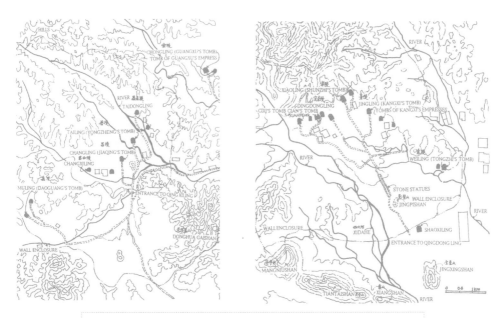

Figure 50 – (above left) Sketch of aerial view of the Eastern tombs of the Qing emperors; (right) Sketch of aerial view of the Western tombs

Glossary
Appendix
Further Reading

Glossary

Azure Dragon   one of the four symbols derived from the *Tai Ji*. A mythical guardian of good report, it represents the physical features on the left side of a site.

Black Turtle   one of the four symbols derived from the *Tai Ji*. It represents the physical features at the back of a site.

cosmic breath   the breath of life for the dead which the Chinese believe to be essential for the wellbeing of the buried

dili jia   a specialist who divines the future by observing the geographical features of a site; *dili* means 'geography'

diqi   earth energy

dui   one of the Eight Trigrams indicated by one broken line and two solid lines. It denotes west, and signifies the clouds and moisture.

Eight Trigrams   ancient philosophers used the Eight Trigrams to represent the eight phenomena—the sun, the earth, thunder, the wind, the watercourse, fire, the hill and the valley. The Trigrams are *qian, kun, zhen, kan, gen, xun, li* and *dui*.

feng shui   *feng* means 'wind' and *shui*, 'water'. Feng shui refers to the natural forces and it is an art of placement of structures on sites so that they are in harmony with the surrounding natural and man-made elements.

Five Elements   everything under the sky can be classified under the Five Elements: Gold, Wood, Water, Fire and Earth. The Elements react with each other in either a destructive or productive manner.

Ganzi   the Chinese calendar is based on the *Ganzi* (Stems and Branches) system in which the *Gan* (the Ten Heavenly Stems) are combined with the *Zi* (the Twelve Earthly Branches) to form the cyclical 60 lunar recurrent years. The *Ganzi* system is devised so that each year is associated with a horoscopic animal symbol.

gen   one of the Eight Trigrams indicated by one solid line and two broken lines. It refers to mountains and the northeast.

geomancer   one who specialises in the art of diving the future from the geographical or directional features of a tomb or building

gua Trigram

Gujin Tushu Jicheng book containing records from ancient to present times

kan one of the Eight Trigrams indicated by a solid line sandwiched by two broken lines. It indicates danger and refers to the north.

kun one of the Eight Trigrams shown as three broken lines. It represents the earth, femininity and the southwest.

li one of the Eight Trigrams denoted by a broken line sandwiched by two solid lines. It is associated with the sun, lightning and fire.

long dragon, a symbol of the beneficial forces of nature. It represents the topography of the land.

luopan a geomancer's compass which contains many rings of information with a magnetic needle at its centre. Among other things, it gives readings directions, orientations, types of water courses, and the positions of Trigrams.

Luoshu Tu the Book of Luo. It is the name given to the diagram created when the yin and yang dots and the Trigrams were drawn to relate to the directions and the Five Elements.

lupan chi a geomancer's ruler divided into eight divisions, each depicting auspicious or inauspicious readings. The geomancer uses it to assess the measurements of doors and furniture.

magic diagrams a nine-square grid which feng shui experts rely on. It reveals the changes in feng shui cycles every 20 years.

minggua *ming* means 'fate' and *gua* means 'Trigram'. The feng shui of a place can be assessed by using the *Minggua* Method. Also means 'horoscope'.

mintang courtyard

qi the energy of the earth, which can be positive and rejuvenating

qian one of the Eight Trigrams denoted by three solid lines. It siginifies the heavens, masculinity and the northwest.

Red Bird one of the four symbols derived from the *Tai Ji*. It represents the physical features in front of a site.

sha sand; in feng shui, it represents the environment of the site.

shaqi literally, 'breath that hurts'; in feng shui, it is overly or excessively vibrant energy

shengqi vibrant and positive energy

siqi stifling energy

Tai Ji *tai* means 'infinity' and *ji*, 'extremity'. Ancient philosophers created this term to represent the origins of things. *Tai Ji* gave birth to yin and yang elements and from it the Eight Trigrams were derived.

Ten Heavenly Stems each of the 60-year cycles in the Chinese calendar consists of a Heavenly Stem and an Earthly Branch. For example, the year *Jiazi* is made up of a unit of the Heavenly Stem named *Jia* and a unit of the Earthly Branch named *Zi*. The Ten Heavenly Stems are *jia*, *yi*, *bing*, *ding*, *wu*, *ji*, *geng*, *xin*, *ren* and *kui*. Also known as *Tian Gan*, a term introduced by the Chinese for things related to Heaven.

tuqi energy from the ground

Twelve Earthly Branches also known as *Di Zhi*, a term introduced by the Chinese for things related to the Earth. The Earthly Branches are *zi*, *chou*, *yin*, *mao*, *chen*, *si*, *wu*, *wei*, *shen*, *you*, *shu* and *hai*.

White Tiger one of the mythical guardians of good report. Derived from the *Tai Ji*, it represents the physical features on the right side of a site.

xue the built up area of a structure, including the foundation

xun one the Eight Trigrams shown as two solid lines and one broken line. It indicates the southeast and the wind.

yin/yang the negative and positive principles in nature. Yin refers to feminine qualities: the moon, the night, the valley etc, whilst yang refers to masculine qualities: the sun, the day, the hill etc. When there is harmony of yin and yang, there is balance and wellbeing.

yinqi moon energy

yangqi sun energy

yun age or era. It is believed that every person experiences lucky and unlucky spells during his or her lifetime. These periods are known as *yun* cycles.

zhen one the Eight Trigrams represented by two broken lines and a solid line. It indicates change and the east.

Appendix 1

The charts below show the roof plan of houses and how feng shui is said to affect the occupants. It is based on data and information obtained from the *Imperial Encyclopedia*, which was written in classical Chinese, and other sources.

Shape of building	Omen	Effect of feng shui
	Good	Wealth will be accrued, but the occupants will not have the blessing of descendants.
	Good	Wealth will be accumulated and riches will be enjoyed.
	Bad	Descendants will be unintelligent and wealth will not be enjoyed.
	Bad	Descendants will not survive. Death will occur in the family.

Shape of building	Omen	Effect of feng shui
stream / N	Bad	The family can obtain riches at an early stage of life but will experience poverty later on.
mound / N	Good	Descendants will be fortunate even though they meet with failure at an early stage of life.
N	Good	Sons will be officials of the government and daughters will be married to well-established officals.
N / hill	Good	Members of the family will be strong, healthy and well established.

Shape of building	Omen	Effect of feng shui
graveyard / N / forest / grave	Bad	Site is unfortunate as it is disturbed by evil spirits. The family will suffer illness.
mountain / N	Bad	Poverty will be suffered for generations. The family will be isolated and lonely.
road / road / road / road / N	Bad	Large sums of money have to be spent to combat malevolent forces and evil influences.

Shape of building	Omen	Effect of feng shui
road ↓ N	Bad	Likelihood of frequent thefts. The family will suffer failure in all their endeavours.
high ground all round ↓ N	Good	Good site for farming. The family will enjoy wealth and highly respectable positions in society.
mountain front ↓ N	Bad	Very unlucky site. The family will not be blessed with descendants.

Shape of building	Omen	Effect of feng shui
alluvial earth north and south ... N	Good	Good harvest of crops for farmers. The family will be blessed with descendants.
N ... stream	Bad	Bad site for farmland. Death and calamity will befall the family, and family members will suffer physical injuries. Even though riches may be enjoyed at the early stage, poverty will befall the family later.
N ... pool	Bad	Family will suffer poverty.

The following drawings are derived from the *Yang Zhai Shi Shu* (the Ten Books on Dwellings of the Living). They show the good and bad layouts of building structures.

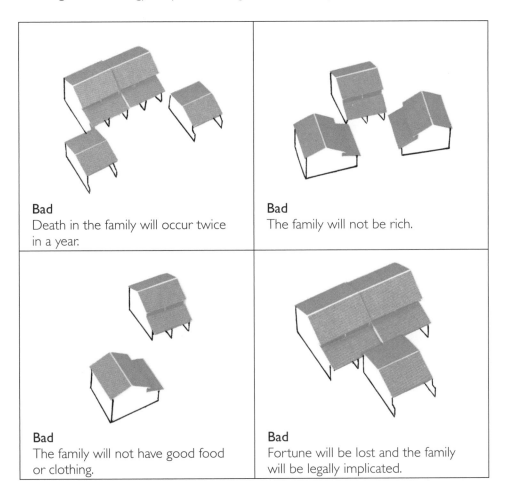

Bad
Death in the family will occur twice in a year.

Bad
The family will not be rich.

Bad
The family will not have good food or clothing.

Bad
Fortune will be lost and the family will be legally implicated.

Bad
The middle block is taller than the
front and rear; the owner is lonely.

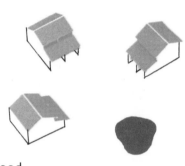

Good
The family will be scholastically
inclined and successful.

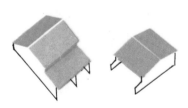

Bad
The family will have shortage of food
and clothing.

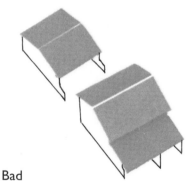

Bad
Young members of the family
will meet with death.

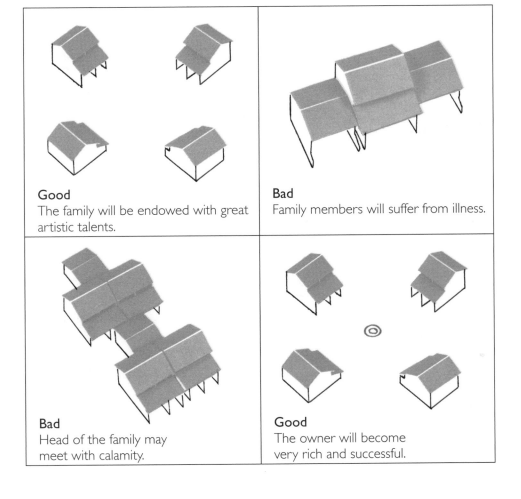

Good
The family will be endowed with great artistic talents.

Bad
Family members will suffer from illness.

Bad
Head of the family may meet with calamity.

Good
The owner will become very rich and successful.

Appendix 2

The following situations are regarded as being unfavourable. They are derived from the *Water Dragon Classic* (AD 600). The dot represents the house while the lines are water courses.

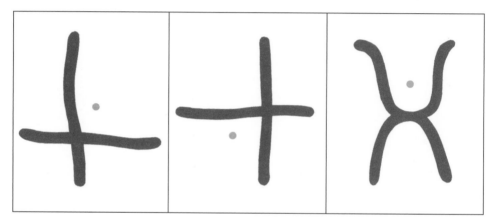

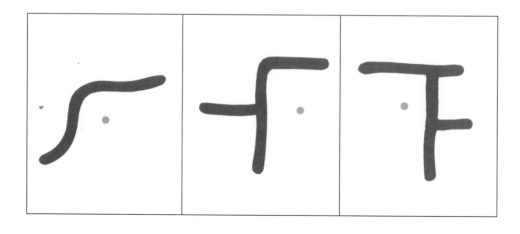

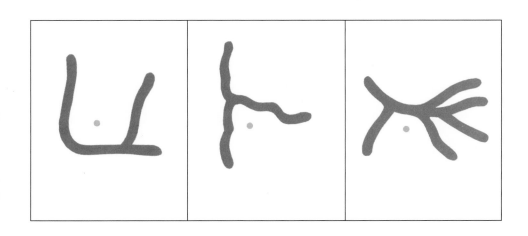

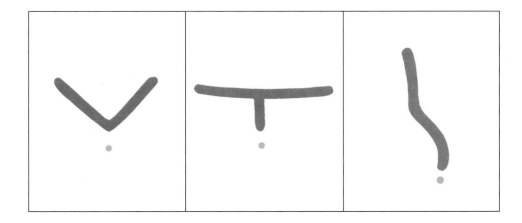

The following diagrams are also derivedfrom the *Water Dragon Classic*. The dot represents the house while the lines are water courses.

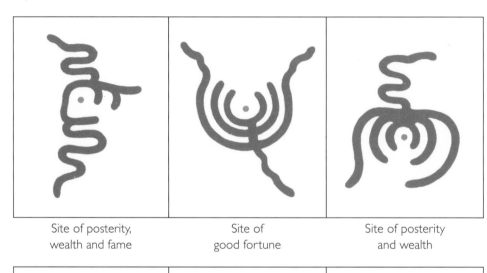

| Site of posterity, wealth and fame | Site of good fortune | Site of posterity and wealth |

| Site of posterity, fame and fortune | Site of wealth and prosperous well-being | Site of posterity and wealth |

Site of great wealth
and posterity

Site of posterity
and wealth

Site of
posterity

Site of
fame

Site of
greatness

Site of posterity,
fame and fortune

Appendix 3

Table showing the relationship between one's Year of Birth and Natal Trigram

Year of Birth	Natal Trigram (Male)	Natal Trigram (Female)		Year of Birth	Natal Trigram (Male)	Natal Trigram (Female)
1930	dui	gen		1953	kun	gen
1931	qian	li		1954	kan	Kun
1932	kun	kan		1955	li	qian
1933	xun	kun		1956	gen	dui
1934	zhen	zhen		1957	dui	gen
1935	kun	xun		1958	qian	li
1936	kan	gen		1959	kun	kan
1937	li	qian		1960	xun	kun
1938	gen	dui		1961	zhen	zhen
1939	dui	gen		1962	kun	xun
1940	qian	li		1963	kan	gen
1941	kun	kan		1964	li	qian
1942	xun	kun		1965	gen	dui
1943	zhen	zhen		1966	dui	gen
1944	kun	xun		1967	qian	li
1945	kan	gen		1968	kun	kan
1946	li	qian		1969	xun	kun
1947	gen	dui		1970	zhen	zhen
1948	dui	gen		1971	kun	xun
1949	qian	li		1972	kan	gen
1950	kun	kan		1973	li	qian
1951	xun	kun		1974	gen	dui
1952	zhen	zhen		1975	dui	gen

1976	qian	li		1999	kan	kun
1977	kun	kan		2000	li	qian
1978	xun	kun		2001	gen	dui
1979	zhen	zhen		2002	dui	gen
1980	kun	xun		2003	qian	li
1981	kan	gen		2004	kun	kan
1982	li	qian		2005	xun	kun
1983	gen	dui		2006	zhen	zhen
1984	dui	gen		2007	kun	xun
1985	qian	li		2008	kan	gen
1986	kun	kan		2009	li	qian
1987	xun	kun		2010	gen	dui
1988	zhen	zhen		2011	dui	gen
1989	kun	xun		2012	qian	li
1990	kan	gen		2013	kun	kan
1991	li	qian		2014	xun	kun
1992	gen	dui		2015	zhen	zhen
1993	dui	gen		2016	kun	xun
1994	qian	li		2017	kan	gen
1995	kun	kan		2018	li	qian
1996	xun	kun		2019	gen	dui
1997	zhen	zhen		2020	dui	gen
1998	kun	gen				

Completed in 1989, this stunning pyramid graces the courtyard of the Louvre Musuem in Paris and serves as the museum's main entrance. It is built mainly in glass and metal, and its shape is of Fire Element.

Further Reading

Ball, Dyer. *Things Chinese*. 4th Edition, London, 1904

Bring, Mitchell & Wayembergh, Josse. *Japanese Garden Design and Meaning*. McGraw Hill, New York, 1981

Creei, H. G. *Chinese Thought*. London, 1954

De Barry, Chan Wing Tsit & Watson, B. *Sources of Chinese Tradition*. London, 1960

De Groot, J. J. M. *The Religious System of China*. Leyden, 1892

Eitel, E. J. *The Rudiments of Natural Science in China*. Hong Kong, 1973

Forlag. *Chinese Buddhist Monasteries*. London, 1937

Graham, David. F*olk Religion in S. W. China*. Washington, 1961

Lai Chuen Yan. "A Feng Shui Model As A Location Index", Annals of the Association of American Geographers. Vol. 64, No. 4

Needham, Joseph. *Science and Civilization in China*. Cambridge University Press, Cambridge, 1982

Pietro, Nancy Santo. *Fengshui Harmony by Design*. Perigee Book, New York, 1996

Yoon, Hong-key. *The Culture of Fengshui in Korea*. Lexington Books, U.K., 2006

SELECTED BOOKS AND ARTICLES BY EVELYN LIP

Chinese Beliefs and Superstitions. Graham Brash, Singapore, 1985

Chinese Numbers: Significance, Symbolism and Traditions. Times Editions Singapore, 1992

Chinese Temples and Deities. Times Books International, Singapore, 1981

Choosing Auspicious Chinese Names. Times Editions, Singapore, 1988

"Feng Shui, Chinese Colours and Symbolism", *Singapore Institute of Architects Journal*, Singapore, 1978

Feng Shui For Harmony In The Home. Marshall Cavendish International (Asia), Singapore, 2008

Feng Shui For Success In Business. Marshall Cavendish International (Asia), Singapore, 2008

Feng Shui In Chinese Architecture. Marshall Cavendish International (Asia), Singapore, 2008

"Geomancy and Building", *Development and Construction*, Singapore, 1977

Notes on Things Chinese. Graham Brash, Singapore, 1988

Out of China, Culture and Traditions. Addison-Wesley, Singapore, 1993

Personalise Your Feng Shui And Transform Your Life. Marshall Cavendish International (Asia), Singapore, 2008

The Design and Feng Shui of Logos, Trademarks and Signboards. Heain International Inc., 1998